Project Plans for All Around the House

Edited by: Jean E. Attebury

Build it Yourself	2
House of Built-ins	3
Garage Units	8
Workshops	10
Kitchens	18
Hideaway Kitchen	19
Preparation Centers	23
Planning Areas	32
Baking Centers	35
Islands of Space	39
Microwave Niches	43
Eating Areas	47
Sew Easy	48
Serving in Style	58
Serving Carts	59
Bars	61
Buffets	62
Shelves and Cabinets	65
Everything in its Place	74
Desks Plus	75
Bookcases/Wall Units	82
Sheer Comfort	90
Bed and Bath	91
Entertainment Centers	98
Entertainment Room	99
Component Units	103
Furniture	114
Oriental Room	115
Seating Arrangements	118
Table Ideas	121
Ordering Information	126

In addition to general descriptions of the projects included in this book, complete plans, instruction details and materials lists are available for all projects. Order forms for these plans are included for your convenience.

Order Forms 127

From the pages of **Better Homes and Gardens®**

BUILD IT YOURSELF

LOCATING YOUR HOME WORKSHOP

If you're going to do it right when you do it yourself, you're going to need a place to work. Basements, garages and attics are all fine candidates for home workshops. But, if you have a basement, that should be your number-one option. A basement is away from living spaces so you need not worry too much about disrupting family activities as you work. It's also one of the few areas in most homes with sizable amounts of unused space. Finally, a basement offers a comfortable environment in which to work — moderately warm in winter, pleasantly cool in summer.

Garages can make good workshop spaces, but you'll have to provide heat, insulation and power if none already exists. In a two-car garage, consider partitioning off part of the space so you'll still have space for one car.

Attics are your final choice for a workshop if no suitable alternative is available. But make certain that the joists supporting the floor are large enough to handle the strain. A contractor or home inspector can tell you if you'll have to beef up the joists to handle the extra load.

Having adequate power for tools is another important consideration. Use extension cords only when absolutely necessary, and choose heavy-duty cords. If your are inexperienced in electrical work, have a professional install outlets and safety devices such as ground fault interrupters, which prevent deadly shocks. The interrupter works as a backup to each outlet's grounding circuit.

A home workshop should have 20-amp circuits for power tools. If possible, lights should be on their own circuits. This is a safety consideration; should a power tool overload a circuit, you won't be caught in the dark while blades or wheels might still be whirling.

You can begin by building yourself a workbench from any of those in this section and then go on to other projects that your family needs around the house. You might even tackle these next built-in furniture projects that will let you squeeze every bit of useable space from your home, no matter how crowded it might currently appear.

1 BANQUETTE DESK: Tuck this handy combination into the corner of a room where you need dining space and a planning desk. The table shown is simply a piece of plywood anchored to a large antique crock. Plan #50421

2 BUILT-IN SOFA: Not only is the entire back of this sofa fitted with shelf space, but additional cubicles are dished out of the front of both end units. The sofa seats five comfortably. Plan #50422

4 House of Built-ins

3 BUILT-IN BEDROOM: Lots of storage and comfort are packed into this bedroom. Low built-ins line the walls and the master bed has four storage drawers underneath. Plan #50423

6 House of Built-ins

HOUSE OF BUILT-INS

In the 26 × 26 foot activity room, as well as in the sleeping wing, the accent is on built-ins. Many of these same ideas can be incorporated into most homes with just a little planning, some simple tools and a modicum of carpentry skills.

A multipurpose room is the spacious heart of today's compact floor plans. The room is actually several rooms in one: the living area, entertainment center, kitchen (located behind the fireplace), and dining space all share the same space but are separate, distinct areas. The focal point of this 676 square foot room is the central fireplace. Though it's not particularly wide, it does a yoeman job of screening the kitchen from view.

Curled in front of the fireplace is the cozy built-in sofa from page 3. The entire surface is painted plywood, decked out with homemade pillows. Traffic flows past the back of the sofa from the entry toward the dining area.

Tucked into the back corner of the multipurpose room are the built-in banquette and planning desk also shown on page 3. The desk has shelves above and drawers below.

The sleeping wing of the house is separated from the living quarters by a five foot buffer zone which includes the utility room and coat closet which both help to isolate sounds from the active side of the house. Two bedrooms and two bathrooms comprise the quiet zone. The back room is set up as a kid's lair, but also could be used as a den, TV room, home office or guest bedroom. At the front end is the master suite — a bedroom, bath and walk-in closet — all sealed off by a privacy door.

In the master bedroom virtually every corner has something built into it. As illustrated on pages 4 and 5, the bed is snuggled into the corner and flanked by low, open-front niches that house the usual bedside necessities. Continuing in both directions from the bed are wall-hugging storage cabinets. These low built-ins are fitted with flip-down fronts that close against invisible magnetic catches.

These custom furnishings will not only make the spaces in your present home much more efficient, but they will also create a clean, coordinated look throughout. Instead of moving to a larger home or going to the expense of adding on, it might be better to add in these built-ins which actually seem to create space.

1 AUTO EQUIPMENT STORAGE: Overall dimensions of this three-part unit are 6' high by 7' wide by 18" deep. The top cabinet is wall hung and designed to hold oil, antifreeze, and cleanup equipment. Below it is the mobile tool cart complete with flip-up lid that serves as a worktop when open. The third section holds tires and tune-up gear. Construction is all butt jointed 3/4 inch plywood. Plan #50227

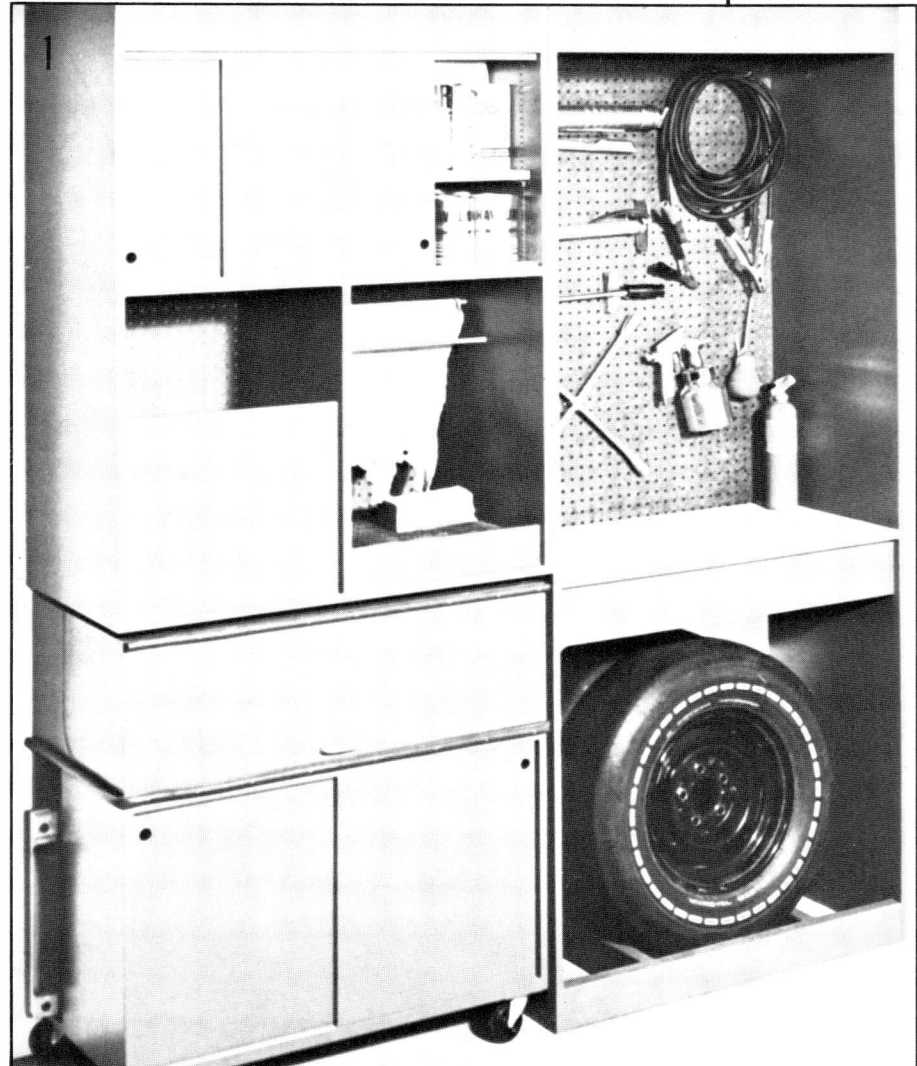

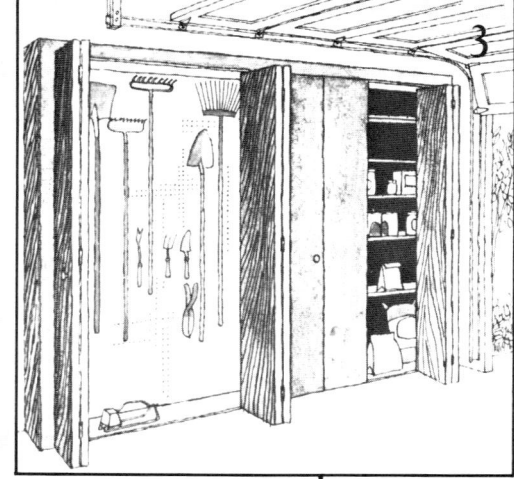

2 FOLD-UP STORAGE: The end section of this handy organizer pulls up out of the way when loaded with out-of-season equipment. The little bench gives you a work surface, then closes and locks to protect hand tools. Garden tools are organized along the big board. Plan #50052

3 SPACE-SAVER STORAGE: This unit tucks a couple of shallow storage closets against the garage wall in recess beside the door. Put shelves on one side for items like paint cans, sprayers, garden supplies and tools. Hanging space in the other section will house rakes, spades, shovels, and all hanging tools. Plan #50101

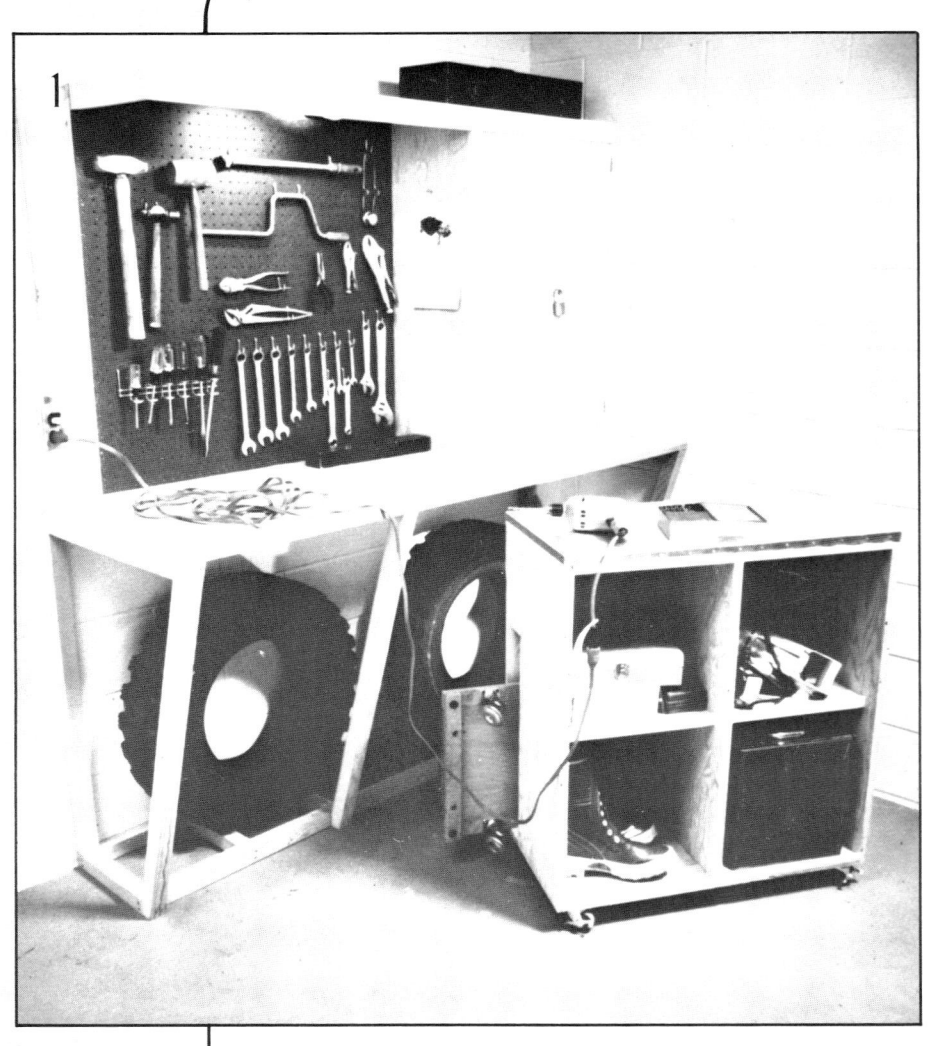

1 WORKBENCH AND COMPANION ROLL-AROUND UNIT: With this unit you can quickly put your hands on just the right tool. Plenty of work space and a tool board are all within easy reach. Wheel the mobile unit right to the job or use it as an auxiliary work surface. Plan #50342

2 TABLE AND COMPANION CABINET: This rugged, well-designed worktable is every handyman's dream. Partner it with this heavy-duty storage cabinet, and you have the best workshop around. Plan #50396

3 OUTDOOR WORK-SHOP: Divided into three sections, this workshop also includes space for storage and shelters enough wood for the entire winter. One room opens with double doors to make a bike port and storage area for a lawnmower or other bulky equipment. The basic framework of 2×4s is covered with cedar-surfaced fir plywood. Get all of the sawdust and all of your tools out of the house and into this spacious shop. Plan #50045

4 WORKSHOP/HOBBY CENTER: In just one 12×16 foot area you can build a 16 foot workbench, two hobby centers, a spray booth and even a cleanup area. It's just what you need if your family has several projects all going at once. Plan #50355

5 MOBILE WORKBENCH: This take-it-to-the-job workbench is a compact 2×4×3 foot. Drawers on both sides hold plenty of tools and other work materials so you'll be able to make all those repairs on the spot. Plan #50427

6 WORKBENCH: This 8×2 foot workbench puts everything at your fingertips and protects your small projects from sawdust and dirt. A 24 inch section of the work surface opens to reveal a dust-free space that's perfect for soldering and other detail work — and for storing precision tools. Although designed for a height of 42 inches, you can custom-fit it to your own needs. As a rule of thumb, make the top of the bench even with the top of your pelvic bone, so you can work comfortably without bending over.
Plan #50283

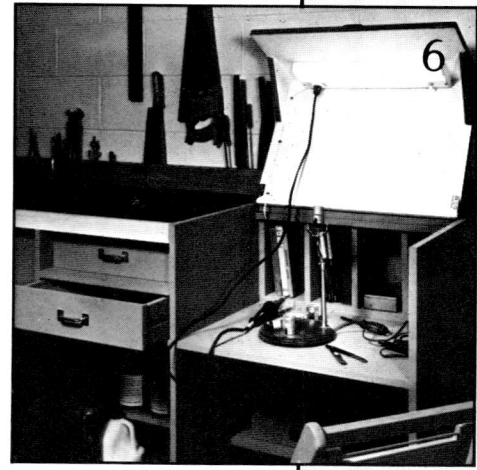

Workshops 15

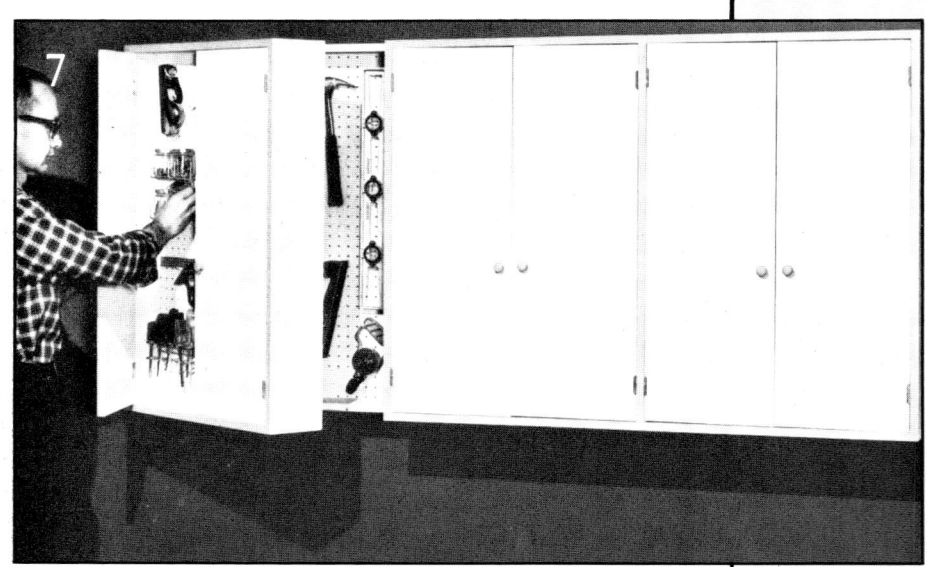

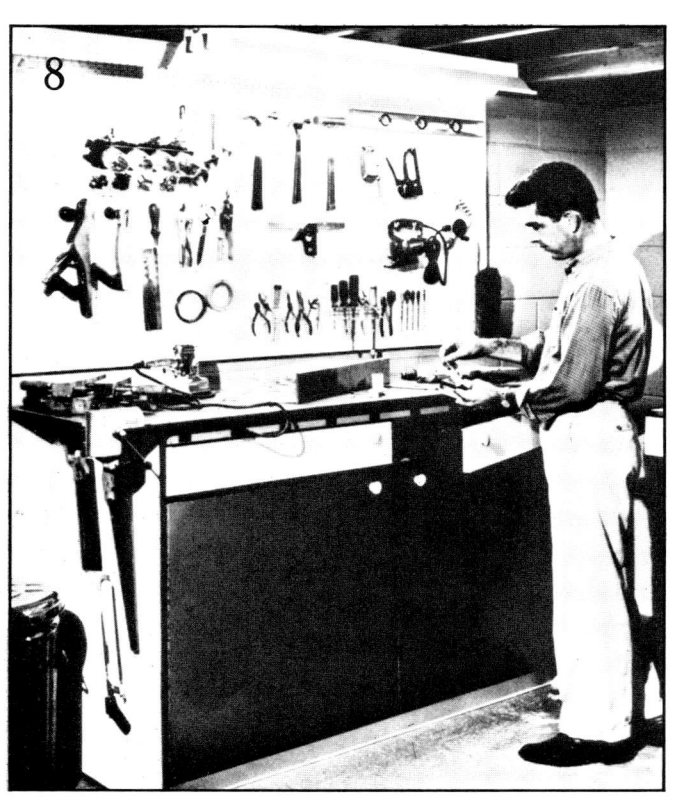

16 Workshops

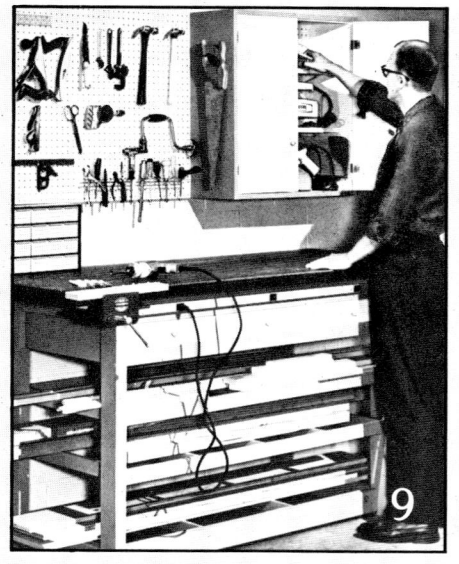 

7 WORKSHOP STORAGE CABINET: The tool board in the end of this hanging cabinet holds an amazingly large selection. Neatly hidden behind is space for storing heavier, less-used tools. Other sections have adjustable shelves. This easy-to-build project will make it simple to organize all your workshop gear. Plan #50066

8 COMPACT WORKBENCH: Several quick cuts of plywood make the basic box for this inexpensive workbench. The doors conceal deep shelves, rather than drawers, and they swing out to make all contents easily accessible. Plan #50039

9 TOOL BOARD AND MATERIALS RACK: Make your shop work better with this neat arrangement. Drawers under the bench top store smaller hand tools, while the board and cabinet take charge of other hand and power tools. The wood grid hold lots of scrap lumber neatly out of the way. Plan #50065

10 FOLD-UP WORKBENCH: If you're looking for a place to keep your tools and equipment well organized in a limited space, try this idea. The two lower doors swing out to support the bench top which swings down. When closed the unit extends only 8″ beyond the wall. Plan #50022

KITCHENS

OPEN KITCHEN, HIDDEN STORAGE

A good house is no better than its kitchen. The kitchen must be a place where you can work and relax at the same time. It must provide an atmosphere that makes cooking creative rather than tedious. It must be warm and inviting for family and friends. It should reflect your personality and personal tastes. And, it has to be easy to keep clean if it's going to work for you.

These are heavy responsibilities for any space to measure up to. Additionally, a kitchen has to house more appliances, more electrical equipment, and more odds and ends in the forms of utensils, pots, pans, dishes, glasses, and other things that can't be stored somewhere else in the house. With all those factors to consider, you might think that designing the ideal kitchen is an impossible task.

A good kitchen designer knows better than that, though. What the kitchen must do determines what it will look like. The key is recognizing the two most critical elements and capitalizing on them throughout the planning process. These elements are open space and hidden storage. No matter how compact the kitchen is, it must give an illusion of expansiveness. One of the best techniques that helps to achieve this effect is to allow one space to borrow from another. For this kitchen, whose features are detailed on the following four pages, kitchen and dining areas occupy the same room. Both feel as large as the total enclosure, although each really occupies just half the space defined by the walls.

For the kitchen to work its best, all appliances and utensils must be within easy reach. This is simple to achieve in an open-storage kitchen, but the ultimate effect often is one of clutter. And, clutter steals from the feeling of openness that is the other element critical to good design.

The solution presented here is to utilize the principles of open storage, but to keep the storage shelves, nooks, and crannies tucked away behind the louvered doors. The work centers are basically closets programmed to work, as well as to store items. The doors are standard closet doors available, along with the rest of the hardware, from most home centers. Complicated joinery is at a minimum, so hand tools or portable power tools can be used in all phases of construction.

Out of sight, out of mind, but always within reach. That's probably the best way to describe every aspect of this kitchen. In fact, the kitchen is really a collection of many mini work centers tucked away along one wall.

This kitchen includes a baking center, a surprisingly large pull-out pantry, a china closet and a hideaway bar. If you plan to adapt this idea to your present kitchen, make certain that these centers are not too far removed from your oven or your sink. Always plan around the traditional work-triangle.

These mini work centers will organize appliances and utensils as well as localize most cooking projects. And best of all, if the doorbell rings and guests surprise you in the middle of a project, all you need to do is close the louvered doors to make the disarray disappear.

1 CLOSET-SIZED BAKING CENTER: Three U-shaped shelves wrap around the interior workspace to hold utensils and supplies. Deep drawers hold bowls and pans and the vertical racks store baking sheets. Plan #50410

2 CHINA CLOSET PLUS: Small items, such as silverware, all have places in the drawers. Tableware is kept in deep drawers, larger serving pieces in divided spaces beneath the drawers, and linen on racks. Plan #50411

22 Hideaway Kitchen

3 PULL AWAY PANTRY: Just 3' deep and 30" wide, this pantry holds as much as a conventional pantry more than twice its size. Six shelving units slide in and out on heavy-duty drawer glides to take advantage of every available cubic inch of space. Since the shelving pulls out into the light and is accessible from both sides, it's almost impossible to lose track of your kitchen inventory. Plan #50409

4 HIDEAWAY BAR: With drawers for wine storage and cabinets for other beverages, this bar is ideal for easy entertaining. The extra sink also separates this refill traffic from the main sink. Glasses are attractively arranged, within easy reach. There's even room to add a trash compactor with easy access to the outside door. Plan #50412

1 KITCHEN PROJECT: Imaginative design and teak-faced plywood combine for this elegant kitchen cabinet/counter plan. Plenty of work space plus the use of economical construction materials make this work area both organized and attractive. Plan #50079

Preparation Centers 23

2 COUNTER WORK AREA: Efficiency isn't sacrificed for good looks in this kitchen project. Open, framed shelves and utensil racks complement the oak plywood "floating" base cabinets. Plan #50112

3 PULLOUT PANTRY: Even items shelved way at the back are within easy reach in this pullout pantry. All you need are a space 30" wide by 2' deep plus some plywood and rollers. Plan #50095

4 TABLE-STYLE ROOM DIVIDER: This eye-catching work center is designed to bring cook and kibitzers together around the work area without creating big traffic jams. The counter top cantilevers so that three sides form a spacious snack bar and serving counter, and the fourth side houses several storage compartments and a dishwasher. The double-door compartment beneath the sink stores cleaning supplies, and the tall niche next to the dishwasher holds cookbooks and serving trays. Two more compartments are left open for convenient access to frequently used items.

The base and counter-top are $3/4$ inch plywood sheathed in orange laminate. Oak accent strips and edgings soften the high-tech effect of the wire storage bins, stainless steel sink and flush cabinet fronts. Plan #50455

5 COOKING CENTER: This cook center offers more than good looks. It rates an A in efficiency by combining storage and a cooking area near the sink and refrigerator. The cooktop reduces the size of the work triangle, thus saving steps for a busy cook. To help out on storage, the island provides roomy drawers, plus a space-saving pot rack complete with a nifty lid hanger. Note also the handy spice rack mounted on the end poles. The cooktop is vented through the floor, eliminating the need for a hood. Above the cooktop a difuser panel conceals fluorescent tubes.

This center can be built in a workshop but should be assembled in the kitchen, as the unit is too wide to get through most kitchen doors. Begin by building the box that comprises the base of the unit, then nail and glue the box to the frame. The headers across the top hold the unit together. The pans hang on eyebolts and wood blocks which slide back and forth. Make the lid rack with 24 inch bungee cords fastened to the framework with wood screws. Cover the top with laminate. Plan #50368

Preparation Centers 27

7

6 ALL-PURPOSE CENTER: Use it for cooking, baking or any other food preparation task. This center combines them all with its butcher-block top and handy shelves. The pan rack pulls out, as does the partition on which the lids are hung. Plan #50372

7 CUSTOM KITCHEN PROJECT: Great kitchens don't have to be big or costly. This design is clean and functional, with a place for every appliance and every work need. The counters are customized with two different surfaces appropriate for specific tasks; the cabinets are within easy reach, and pots and pans are placed in a usually wasted corner. Plan #50332

Preparation Centers 29

30 Preparation Centers

8 THE CANNERY: Corral all those canning jars, pectin, boxes of paraffin, pressure cookers, water bath canners, and cheesecloth in one tidy cabinet. This cannery center includes a bar sink for washing berries or cucumbers; flip-up leaves on the ends that extend the counter space; plus a backsplash that's easily washable in case you get too enthusiastic with the produce. The laminate top resists blueberry stains and comes clean with a wipe of the sponge. It could even double as a buffet. Plan #50376

9 STEP-SAVING COOKING CENTER: In some kitchens, laying out an efficient work triangle is a problem because the wall space isn't where you need it. One solution is to anchor part of your work triangle on an island. By placing the cooking center midway between the sink and the refrigerator, you can effectively increase your work space and eliminate unnecessary motion.

The base of the unit is fitted with a series of specially designed drawers that put cookware, utensils and supplies within fingertip reach. Deep drawers on one side hold large pots and pans, and glass-fronted drawers along one end store fruits, vegetables, and staples. The see-through drawers make it easy to take inventory, and their contents add an extra touch of color and texture to the work area.

Facing the sink at the opposite end of the unit are four additional drawers, one of which holds a large collection of herbs and spices. The bottom of the spice drawer is divided into upward-slanting sections so that the contents of each section can be viewed at a glance and each bottle can be lifted out easily.

The see-through drawers and the base of the cabinet are framed with oak, and the counter top is constructed of laminated maple. Pewter and oak drawer pulls and the richly carved panel mounted on the far side of the island match those on the cabinets that line the walls. Plan #50458

1 KITCHEN STORAGE WALL: A four-way stretcher, this kitchen storage wall serves a multitude of purposes. Functioning as a planning desk it has plenty of shelves for cookbooks and other materials for planning family menus or complete dinner parties. As a message center there's space for the phone, address books, phonebooks, a space for posting messages, and lots of room for extra pencils. The closed storage areas may store infrequently used appliances or your special silver pieces. Or simply use the extra surfaces for big jobs like decorating all of those Christmas cookies. This is the perfect set-up for those with more organizational skills than space.

Although shown as a built-in, this multipurpose unit may be constructed so as to be freestanding. Based on a simple box-like design, the building process is easy and quickly accomplished. AC-grade interior plywood, plastic laminate, and corkboard are all the materials you'll need to build this versatile and space stretching storage wall for your kitchen. Plan #50203

2 PLANNING CENTER: This jazzy planning center makes mundane bill paying and menu planning more bearable. Build the 2 × 2 island from plywood, paint a bright color, and cover the top with plastic laminate. Plan #50370

1 ONE-STOP BAKING CENTER: Messy chores like kneading bread or rolling out pastry can turn a kitchen topsy turvy, but this unit will consolidate the clutter and contain the mess. Plan #50457

34 Planning Areas

Baking Centers 35

2 THE BAKERY: You'll look forward to getting elbow-deep in flour if you have a bakery center as well decked out as this one. It even has old-fashioned flour and sugar dispensers built into the upper cabinet. Plan #50375

3 BAKE CENTER: Add six square feet of counter space to your kitchen. The simple, straight-forward design of this unit makes it easily adaptable to any type of kitchen layout or work situation. Plan #50456

Baking Centers 37

38 Baking Centers

4 BAKING CENTER: If you're a bread or pastry buff, you'll find this handsome bake center made to order from its marble top to its overhead rack. Deep, ten-pound capacity sugar and flour bins are partitioned to keep sugar and whole wheat, rye and all-purpose flour handy. The rack above keeps baking trays and pans within easy reach. Plan #50371

5 ROLL-AROUND BAKING CENTER: An extra top on this handy storage center flips open to double the work area when needed. Two adjustable shelves and a large, five-inch-deep drawer help you store odd-sized kitchen equipment. Just move it to the handiest location for help with your every baking project. Plan #50430

1 APPLIANCE ISLAND: You can fit all your portable electric appliances into this neat island unit. The outlets ringing the top pedestal let you use several appliances at once. Besides providing extra counter space, the island works as a sit-down planning desk or as a handy place for a quick breakfast or snack. Plan #50117

2

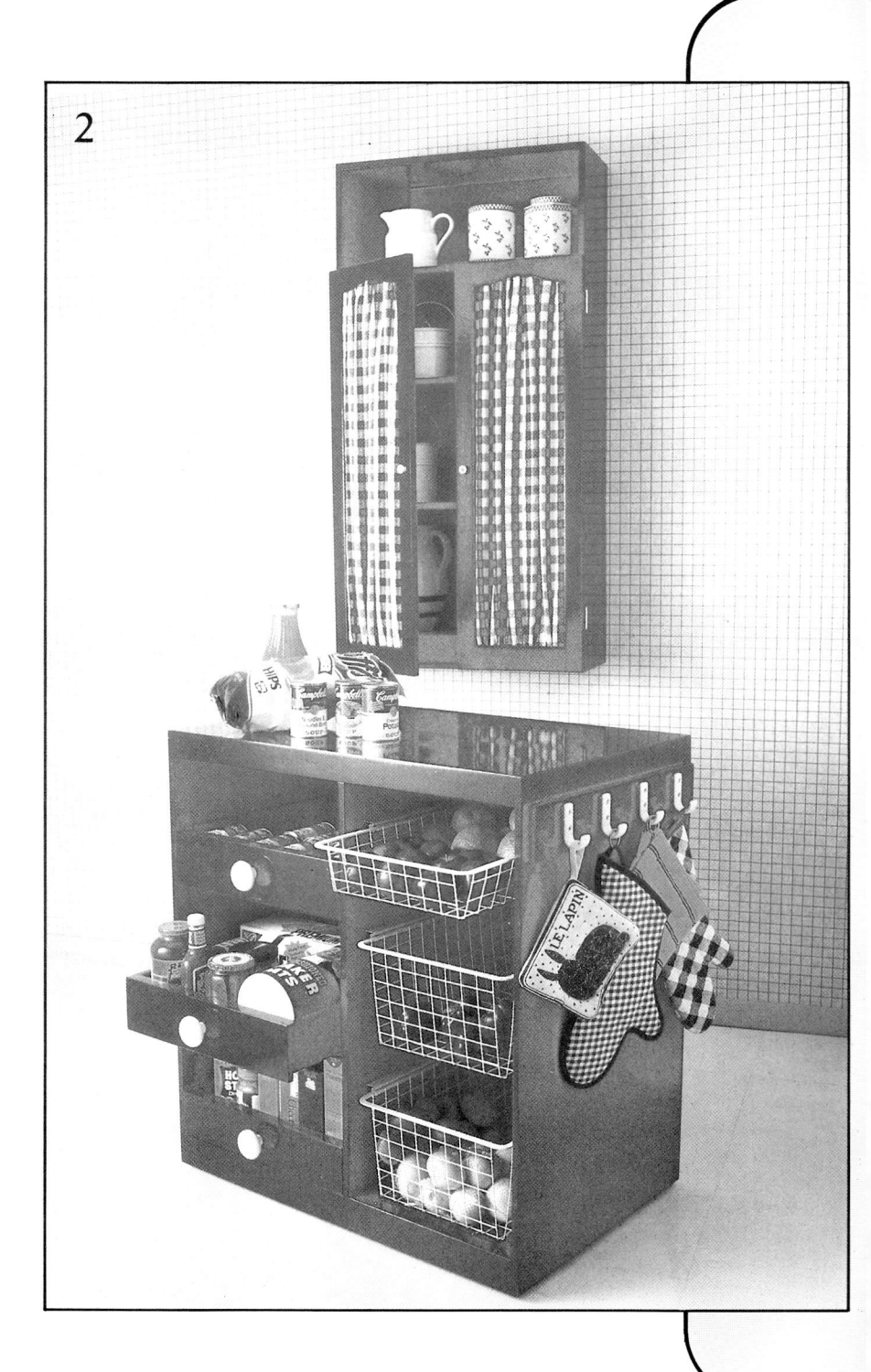

2 MOBILE COUNTER TOP PANTRY: Just wheel this unit to any place you need a little more space in the kitchen and glide it back out of the way when the project is completed. The shelves and the hanging baskets all pull out for easy access to the items at the back. Pot holders are always handy when stored on the decorative hooks lining the ends. Plan #50454

3 QUICK-CHANGE ISLAND: Add extra counter space to your kitchen and build yourself a sewing center at the same time. The top of the island unfolds to make a firm working surface for cutting and sewing. In its unfolded position the top extends beyond the base unit to give ample knee room. Sewing machine and carrying case store in a deep compartment at the end of the cabinet, while pattern and fabrics fit behind the sliding doors.
Plan #50220

Islands of Space 41

Parking your microwave oven on the kitchen counter usually amounts to a trade-off between precious work space and quick-as-a-wink cooking convenience. In most cases there are better alternatives. Some make the space you already have work harder, while others borrow a few square feet from a storage space. With either approach you can incorporate special design features that make your microwave oven more convenient than ever — give it a permanent home, and make your entire kitchen more functional.

1 SUSPENDED MICROWAVE: This microwave oven is built into a large cabinet suspended from the ceiling. The oven sits at eye level above one end of a long peninsula. Work space on the peninsula serves as a staging area for the oven and for the cooktop at the opposite end. Note how the hanging cabinet and the peninsula work as a unit; the oven and dishwasher on the one end and the storage compartments along the side are stacked as if built into a wall. Open shelving on the far side holds table accessories and display items, and recessed fixtures under the shelving supply task lighting for the work surface. Plan #50473

2 ROLL-AROUND MICROWAVE CENTER: This compact cabinet provides space for your microwave oven anywhere it's most convenient. In addition to freeing counter space, this handy mobile unit adds extra storage for lots of hard-to-store pieces of cooking or baking equipment. The pull-out shelf and towel rack put needed accessories within easy reach. Besides the lower cabinet space, the two drawers make finding the right utensil a snap. Plan #50453

Microwave Niches 43

3

3 PIGGYBACK MICROWAVE CUBICLE: This table-style baking center separates the kitchen from the eating area. One end of the unit stairsteps to form a counter-height cubicle for the microwave oven. The three drawers below the microwave are excellent for storing bakeware of all sizes. On the opposite side of the microwave niche is a recessed area for holding canisters. The spacious work surface allows for preparation of large projects or rolling out large amounts of dough. Part of this work area cantilevers over a parking spot designed for a mobile serving cart. Butcher-block work surfaces and oak door and drawer fronts accent the white laminate used to face the sides of the unit.
Plan #50475

46 Microwave Niches

4 ISLAND MICROWAVE NICHE: Carve out some of that floor space and build yourself a handy place for the microwave plus a miniature snack bar. Located within easy reach of the other major appliances, this convenient island provides extra work space and a breakfast or snack bar plus frees up much needed counter space. A special niche cut in one side of the island houses the microwave oven. Because the island doubles as a snack bar, the oven is handy for serve-yourself short orders. A deep drawer below the oven holds mixing bowls, and the butcher-block top provides an easy-to-clean work surface. Plan #50474

1 SERVING BAR: Add informal dining to your kitchen, or provide a convenient place for kibutzers that's friendly, but out of the cook's way, with this nine foot snack bar. The main structure of this easy-to-build serving bar is ¾ inch fir plywood. Easy construction plans even include the overhead light-box. It's the perfect answer to a much needed in-kitchen eating space. Plan #50163

2 BREAKFAST NOOK: A kitchen eatery doesn't have to gobble up your floor space. The restaurant engineering and contemporary country styling of this design will reflect your good taste and your ingenuity. Plan #50210

3 SNACK BAR: Build the convenience of this versatile snack bar into your kitchen. Standard redwood boards, framing 2 × 4s and plywood tops make it a simple weekend project. Plan #50128

Eating Areas 49

SEW EASY

ESPECIALLY FOR SEWING

Even if you love to sew — you doubtless hate the hassle of getting ready to sew. Dragging equipment out of hiding, finding fabric that's stashed here and there, and hunting for pins and thread are all time and energy wasters. Solve these problems — and more — with a single, simple sewing stowaway that also operates as a complete work area.

Here and on the following pages are several sewing centers you can build. Any sewer who's tried to make do with less will tell you — they're invaluable. All you have to do is pick your type and style.

1 SEWING ROOM CONVERSION: An add-on activity room like this sewing center could even fit in the corner of your double garage. Everything from walls to cabinets is detailed in the easy how-to plan. Plan #50158

2 SEWING CABINET: With this unit tucked neatly into a corner, all your sewing needs are ready for use at a moment's notice. Legless cabinets of 3/4-inch plywood allow quick floor cleanup. Plan #50154

3 FOLD-DOWN SEWING CENTER: The tabletop folds up over the shallow cabinet and the legs drop down to form part of the frame around a picture mounted on the underside of the tabletop. It's nearly invisible. Plan #50119

Sew Easy 51

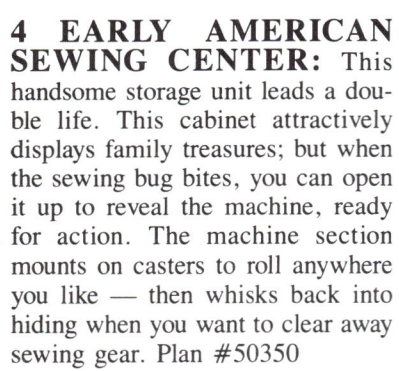

4 EARLY AMERICAN SEWING CENTER: This handsome storage unit leads a double life. This cabinet attractively displays family treasures; but when the sewing bug bites, you can open it up to reveal the machine, ready for action. The machine section mounts on casters to roll anywhere you like — then whisks back into hiding when you want to clear away sewing gear. Plan #50350

5 HI-STYLE SEWING CABINET: Packed into the attractive and contemporary cabinet is a complete sewing center. The separate base unit moves out of the framework; hidden casters provide easy mobility. The roll-around cabinet furnishes support for the drop-down work top; it doubles as a door on the right side of the cabinet. Store fabrics and notions on the plentiful shelves. Plan #50219

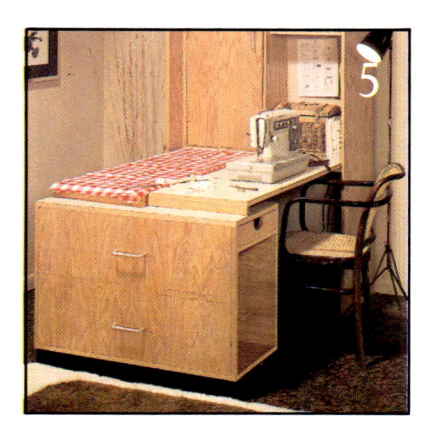

Sew Easy 53

54 Sew Easy

6 MODERN SEWING CIRCLE: This contemporary sewing hideaway would enhance any decor. Because the cabinet doesn't attach to the wall, the entire unit can be moved if you rearrange the furniture. Two big side cupboards house sewing paraphernalia or provide handy storage for games, records, or whatever your family needs to stash away. You can make most of the components from close-grained, 3/4 inch plywood, and use butt joints throughout. The two end doors in the base cabinet operate, but the center two doors are false.
Plan #50351

7 IN-CLOSET LAUNDRY CENTER: Don't forget to add efficiency to taking care of all those items of clothing you've spent so many hours making. This closet-sized laundry center incorporates plenty of convenience in very little space. Laundry duties get much easier with this streamlined center. There's space below for sorting baskets on handy pullout shelves. Then use the top of the dryer and the counter for folding. The open shelves accommodate sewing accessories for mending. Plan #50081

8 SEWING CENTER IN A CLOSET: Everything you need to design and construct complete wardrobes is all packed into this compact closet. Made primarily of 3/4 inch plywood, the closet measures 22 × 32 × 94 inches. When not in use, the sewing table folds back into the cabinet. The table pivots on a metal bar near the door edge; a fold-down panel on the back wall keeps the table secure. Plan #50209

Sew Easy 55

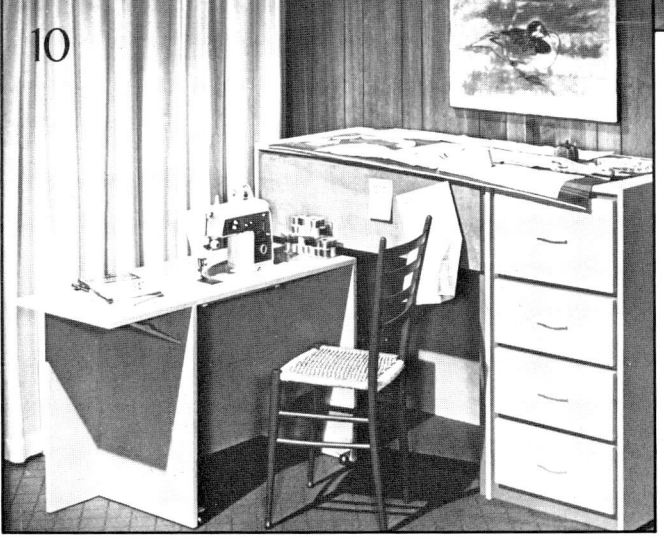

9 BEDROOM CHEST/SEWING CENTER: Just four feet of wall space is needed to turn your bedroom or guest room into a sewing center. Move it away from the wall, swing up the work surface and go to work. Plan #50217

10 SECRET SEWING CENTER: Quickly made of plywood and pine, this compact center also quickly stores any uncompleted projects and hides the clutter. Even the chair stores inside. Plan #50179

11 COMPLETE SEWING CENTER: Designed to store everything you need in a compact area, the shelves, drawers and cabinets hold loose bobbins, patterns and fabric. Close the doors and everything disappears. Plan #50186

12 WORKTABLE/CABINET: The $3 \times 5^{1}/_{2}'$ top is perfect for cutting and each end flips up to reveal plenty of storage. Twin cabinets, $28 \times 18''$, have lots of shelf space behind their sliding doors. Plan #50193

SERVING IN STYLE

HOW TO INSTALL TRACK LIGHTING

Spotlight your treasured china. Dramatically light the centerpiece for your most formal dinner party. Illuminate that wonderful collection of antique glassware. No matter what your lighting needs, you can solve many problems as well as create new decorating options with track lighting.

Versatile track lighting is made to order for contemporary homes, and its installation is well within the ability of most do-it-yourselfers. A variety of connectors is available — T, X, L, straight and rotating, so you can design about any pattern of track you'd like.

The power supply for your system can originate from either a "live-end," which is located at one end of the track, or a "center feed," positioned somewhere along the track. The wiring instructions given here are for a one-circuit system; however, a three-circuit version is also available.

To wire a live-end, first make sure the power supply is disconnected. Cut a hole in the ceiling large enough to accommodate an outlet box. Recess the outlet box in the ceiling. Run wires from a nearby on/off switch behind the wall and ceiling and down through the box. Or install a new switch.

Next, unscrew the cover plate on the bottom of the live-end, insert the wires into the proper terminals, and tighten the screws. With this done, secure the mounting plate to the outlet box and screw the outlet box cover to the mounting plate. Then screw the live-end cover plate back into position and slip the live-end into the outlet box cover.

The first section fits into the live-end. Each succeeding section fits into a connector which fits into the previous section. Cover the end section with a dead end — a plug that covers the copper conductor wires.

If the ceiling surface is even, have a helper position the track sections where you want them, while you drill up through the top of the tracks at various intervals, and mount them to the ceiling with wood screws or toggle bolts. If the surface is uneven, fasten spacer clips to the ceiling first. Position the adapters and the fixtures along the track and light up your room.

1 ROLL-AROUND SERVING CENTER: It's a mobile bar this way, but fold out the leaves and move it against the wall and it's a buffet. Lower the leaves and it sits out of the way disguised as a small chest. Plan #50118

2 STURDY SERVING CART: Assemble this handy roll-about from tongue-and-groove 2×6s edged with 1×2s. Cut the legs from 2×2s, and the wheels from a 2×10. It follows the action anywhere. Plan #50406

Serving Carts 59

3 NOTCH-TOGETHER SERVING CART:
Making this simple cart is a snap. Cut the basic shapes from plywood, notch them together, add casters and a tricycle for mobility and you're ready to party. Plan #50391

4 ROLL-AROUND CENTER:
This portable island is ideal for mixing drinks plus storing the supplies. It also sports drop leaf shelves which flip up for added serving space. Plan #50369

5 PORTABLE BAR:
Entertaining is easier when you store all your party supplies in this 26 × 18 × 31 inch portable bar. It's easily built from just two sheets of 1/2" plywood. Plan #50432

4

5

Bars 61

62 Buffets

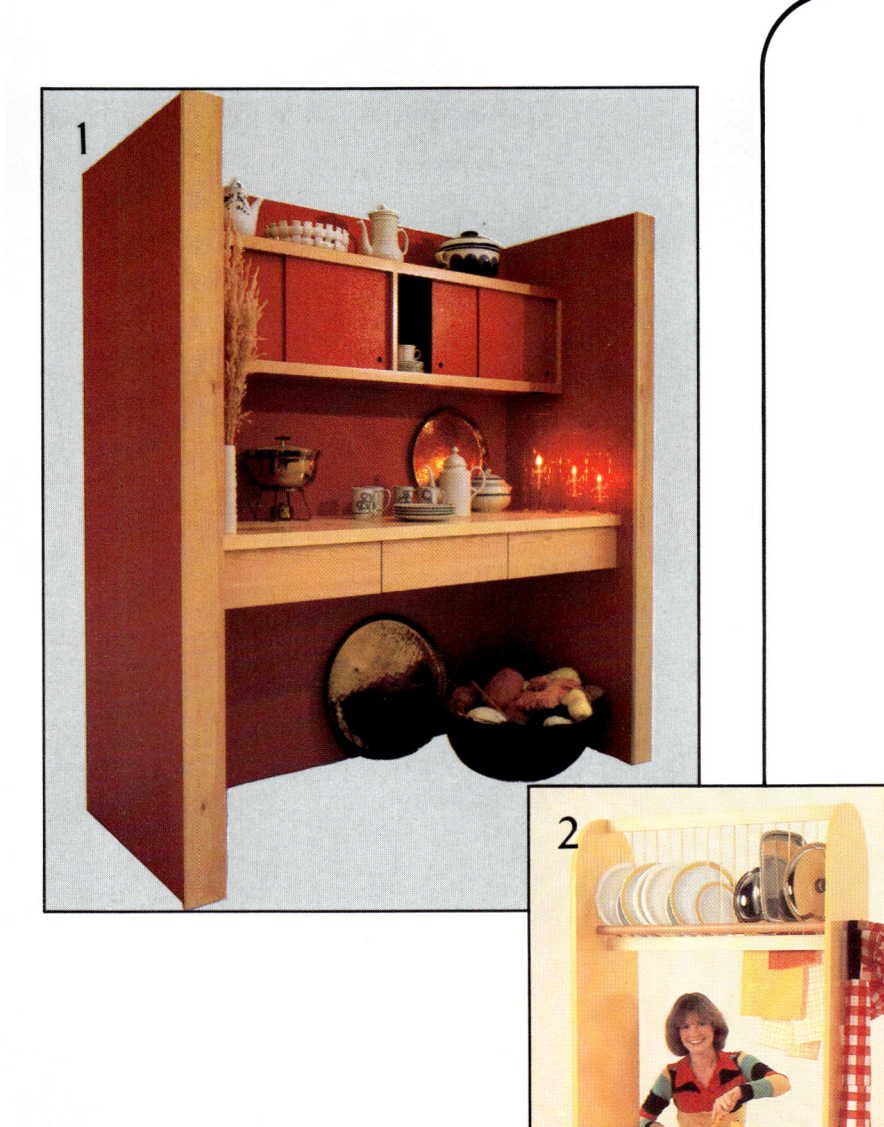

1 DIVIDER BUFFET: This freestanding buffet with sliding doors can help you carve a dining area out of a big room. The shelves and drawers store heaps of linens, china and flatware. Plan #50402

2 SIDEBOARD DIVIDER: This unit makes a handsome divider between food preparation and dining areas and also provides a handy and attractive storage shelf for plates and serving pieces. Plan #50364

3 BUFFET: Solid color, natural wood and ornate brass hardware combine to give this relatively simple buffet a remarkably elegant feeling. The two units that make the buffet, plus the cabinet above, are really just hardwood plywood boxes fitted with drawers and doors. The buffet units are joined by a shallow, laminate-covered top which matches the door and drawer fronts. Plan #50132

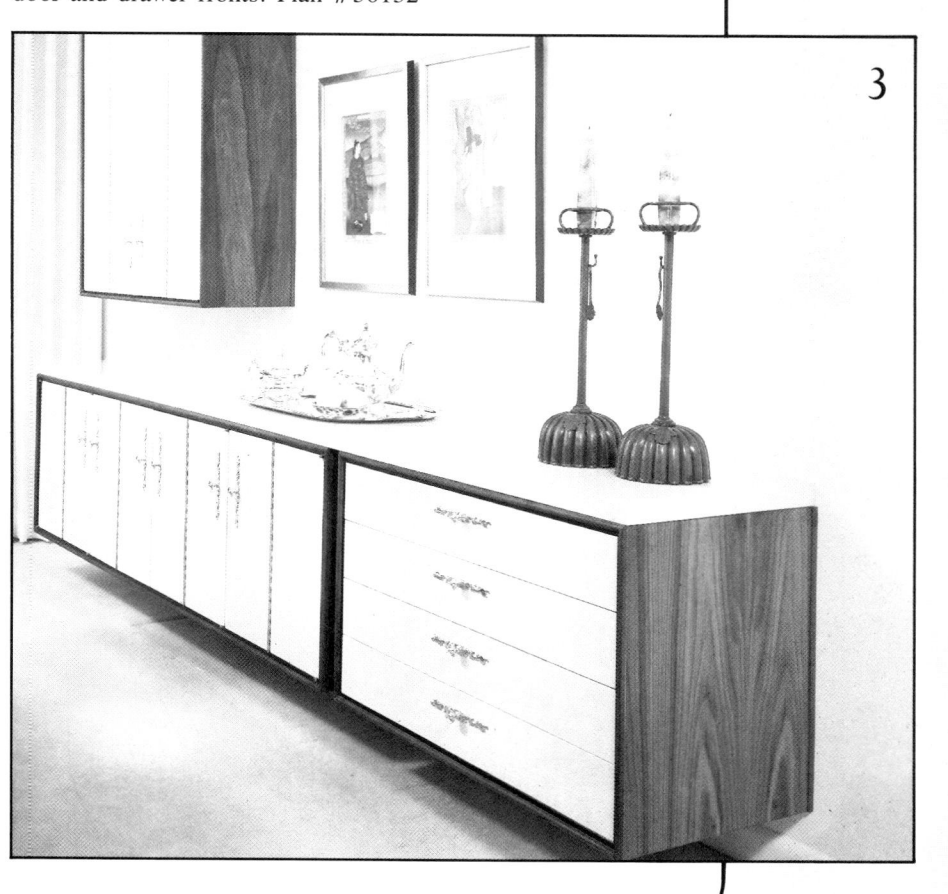

4 WALL-HUNG BUFFET: Simple box construction and stock louvered doors add up to a wall-hung buffet that offers not only a generous serving top, but also plenty of hideaway space for china, linens and silver. Dimensions are determined by door sizes and your own specific needs. Plan #50024

1 FOLD-UP SHELVES: These extra shelves work just the same as a big pine shutter, opening to reveal six $8^1/_2 \times 13^3/_4''$ shelves. The 1×2 control bar acts as a leg when open and hooks into a notch in the upper crosspiece when closed. Plan #50365

Shelves and Cabinets 65

2 CRAFTY CHINA CABINET: Use this unusual cabinet to display your favorite cookbooks or serving pieces. Glued on fabric designs add a folk art touch to this classic design. Finished dimensions are 36 × 23 × 78 inches.
Plan #50401

3 TOO PRETTY TO STOW: Give your loveliest tableware the spotlight it deserves, both on and off the table, with one of these three storage/display units. You'll like what these projects do for a favorite room and for your too pretty-to-put-away china.

Craft this rustic hutch from pine to rekindle that do-it-yourself spirit of the past. Stock the hutch with down-home dishes like these, whose designs were inspired by cross stitch samplers and country quilts.

Build this handsome wall mounted cup rack and fill it with beautiful cups, saucers and other teatime paraphernalia. With your tea set so handy, you can relax and enjoy the polite custom of afternoon tea.

Show off your prettiest silver patterns with this easy-to-build flatware rack. Stand individual pieces handle side up and lean each piece against the notched bar. Adjust the length of this rack to accommodate as many pieces as desired or, build several racks and mount them on the wall.

Don't hide your pretty tableware and silver in a closed cupboard; display it and decorate your dining room at the same time.
Plan #50471

Shelves and Cabinets 67

4 COLONIAL HUTCH: This do-it-yourself reproduction features both authentic styling and commodiou[s] storage. Plan #50386

68 Shelves and Cabinets

5 CAPACIOUS CABINET: Use this spacious cupboard for china and glass storage or fill it with books or audiovisual equipment. Plan #50445

Shelves and Cabinets 69

6

70 Shelves and Cabinets

6 WELSH CUPBOARD: The base of this ultramodern version of a traditional Welsh cupboard is built like a simple table. The top and shelves are made of 1 × 4s. The top section is screwed to the tabletop and attached to the wall for increased stability. Plan #50348

7 WALL-HUNG CHINA DISPLAY: Add a bit of old-time country flavor to your dining area with this simple, yet decorative wall display. Plan #50363

8 PLATE RACK: The handsome pine plate rack is designed for construction in the home workshop. To give the plate rack added importance, it is framed with a simple stencil design. Plan #50357

9 BENCH/COFFEE TABLE: The sleek design of this pine bench highlights its functional adaptability. Here it is used a coffee table, but it may find a home in the kitchen, in the dining room, or even in the den. Simple, classic construction is at home anywhere. Plan #50358

72 Shelves and Cabinets

10 POPLAR BENCH: This clean-lined slatted bench looks smart anywhere, from living room to sheltered porch. Plan #50448

11 POPLAR TABLE: Half-lapped X-shaped legs provide a sturdy base for this smart looking table. Plan #50449

12 GOBLET RACK: Build a simple box of shelves to hold your crystal goblets. You can buy the fancy crest precut or design and cut out your own. Plan #50450

EVERYTHING IN ITS PLACE

HOW TO WORK WITH ARTIFICIAL BRICK VENEER

The rich textures and colors of brick can add a cozy, rustic feel to your family room or den. A wide range of artificial brick veneer is available, so you can enjoy the look of brick without coping with the cost of installation or the weight of the real thing.

Most brands of the artificial brick veneer can be installed over any sound, dry, fairly flat surface — even over masonry. Unless your wall has a moisture problem or a highly irregular surface, you won't have to worry about installing a furring system before you start.

Whether you're working with single units or panels of 12 to 24 bricks, the first step is to lay out the wall in advance. Decide on the pattern you want to establish along the wall and plan how you're going to handle obstructions and openings. Then cut the veneer pieces.

Most brick panels can be nailed or glued to the wall. Some may require mortar. The panels are especially quick and easy to install because they cover large areas, and some brands don't even require application of an adhesive on their back surfaces.

Installing individual bricks is more time consuming, but will yield more design opportunities. Begin by covering only a small area — $2 \times 6'$ — at a time. Spread adhesive on the wall sections first. Then — using a tight, level string as a guide and starting in one corner — build the bottom row of bricks, spreading adhesive onto the back of each brick as you go. Use a spacer between bricks to maintain the uniform gap suggested by the manufacturer.

Proceed up the wall, using either the tight string or a level to guide each row. Handle inside corners as you do the rest of the wall; use the manufacturer's special corner bricks on outside corners. If you get adhesive on the face of a brick, remove it with the specified cleaner.

Some brands require no grouting because the adhesive dries to a gritty, mortarlike texture; others must be grouted. Usually the grouting is done with a caulking gun.

1 THE OFFICE: Small though it is, this unit contains all the amenities necessary for efficient household management: shallow drawers for pens, pencils and stationery; a wall-mounted telephone; open bookshelves for how-to information and cookbooks. There's even a tall closet at the end for brooms, a vacuum and umbrellas. Face the closet door with cork and you have an instant bulletin board.
Plan #50374

2

3

4

76 Desks Plus

2 ENTRY DIVIDER: Organize the entry to your home with this functional divider. Upper shelves can be used to create an attractive display area while the lower cabinets and drawers can alleviate some of the clutter of mail, boots, mittens or other "stuff" that always seems to collect around the front door. This easy-to-build unit solves the problem of designating an entry without building a permanent wall between living areas. Plan #50057

3 SLANT-FRONT DESK: This sturdy oak desk features pigeonholes for compartmentalized storage. The glass-fronted lower storage area holds plenty of supplies or can be used to display knickknacks or your paperweight collection. The desk surface folds up and out of the way when the work is completed, thus saving space and creating an uncluttered appearance. Plan #50447

4 HIDEAWAY DESK: This functional, yet "invisible" desk is just the solution to needing plenty of desk space, but not having room for it. The compact cabinet is only $30 \times 22 \times 28$ inches when closed, but opens into a full-sized desk with storage, drawers and bookshelves. The hinged writing surface folds down between the two halves of the unit when not in use. Plan #50433

Desks Plus 77

5 PIGEONHOLE DESK: A desk need not be an antique rolltop to sport plenty of handy little pigeonholes for eye-level storage. This streamlined version is sturdy, yet practical and will fit into any useable space. There's ample work space for handling all the bills and paperwork that accompany managing a household. Plan #50400

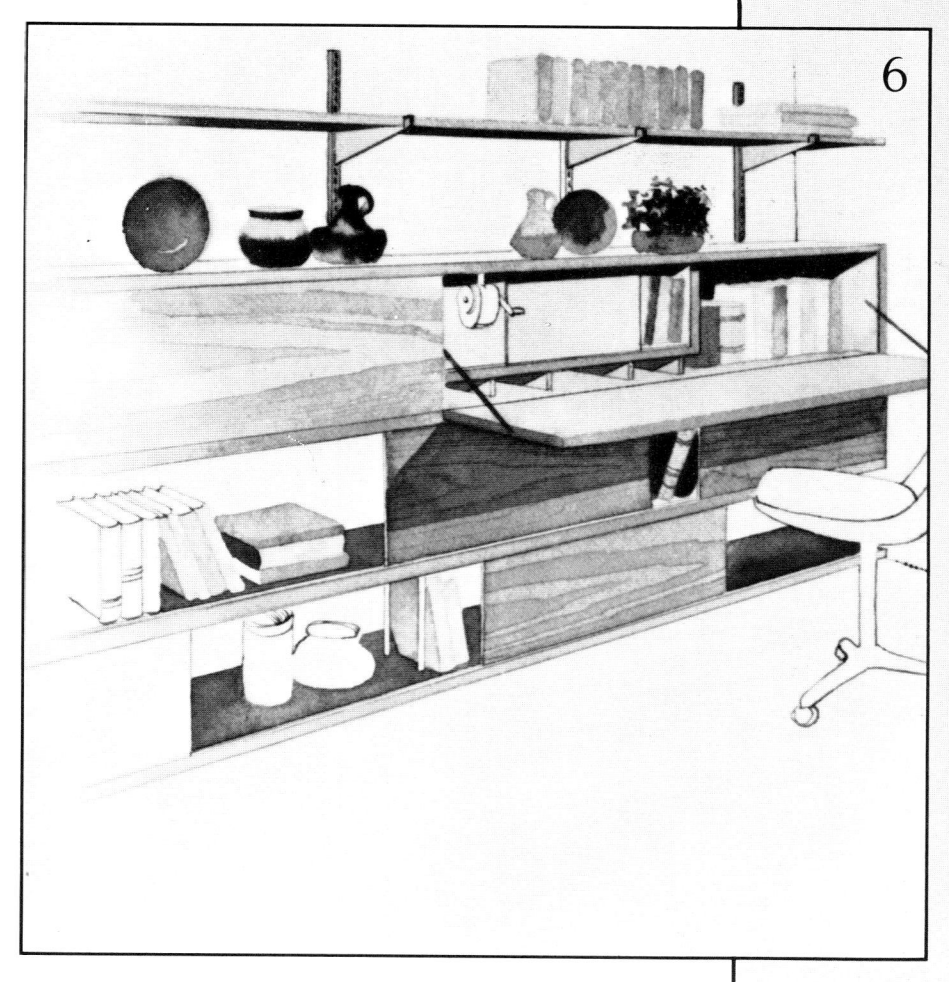

6 DESK/BOOKSHELF UNIT: This sturdy unit is an economical way to turn bookshelf space into a study. It's a great way to keep all of your personal things in one convenient spot and free floor space for leisure-time activities. The fold-down desk top enables you to leave a project at any time without putting everything away. The ample bookshelves may be used for display, for all of those books you intend to read or for handy placement of your reference books.

If you can make a box, the project is a snap. Largely constructed from plywood, this versatile unit can be adjusted to any room or location. You just add sliding doors and a desk top to the basic box and stack the finished products to the desired height. Plan #50053

7

80 Desks Plus

7 ENTRY POST OFFICE: Here's a family post office and desk in one unit that creates order from chaos. It gives you a desk right in your living room, plus plenty of niches for necessary papers. Plan #50116

8 DESK/BOOKCASE: Put a library in your living room using only a few square feet of floor space. Fold-down desk top and storage compartments keep you organized. Plan #50043

1 BOOKCASE BUILT-IN: Here's the perfect answer for an awkward window wall at the end of a room. This built-in bookcase features elegant arches which will add dimension as well as an elegant touch to brighten any room.

The bookcases flanking the window are constructed of 1×10 pine boards. You can construct these units in the room and then stand them in a corner until you're ready to attach them to the wall. Frames are about three inches shorter than ceiling height for ease of handling. This space will eventually be covered by the plywood arches.

The lower cabinet section is built under the windows and should be adjusted to the specific height you need. The arches are then applied, followed by the door which is constructed from 1×2 pine and decorative hardboard. Hang the shutters over the windows and add the adjustable shelves.

These spacious, arched bookcases will give any room in your house a bright, sunny look that will accent any style of furniture or decor. Plan #50027

82 Bookcases/Wall Units

2 ADJUSTABLE BOOKSHELVES: Create the quiet appeal of a library any place in your home with this adaptable unit. This wall of desk/shelf built-ins helps to organize and display family treasures. It also presents a convenient and efficient area in which to study, plan, pay bills, deal with correspondence or write grocery lists while still joining the rest of the family in their activities. As activities change or the room is redecorated, the shelves of this unit can easily be adjusted to accommodate any modifications you might wish to make. Plan #50030

Bookcases/Wall Units 83

3 STORAGE WALL/WORK DESK/COUCH/END TABLES: Build an entire room from this versatile plan. The storage wall has racks for fabrics and pegs for yarns, supplies of hemp or spools of decorative trim. There's lots of extra space provided in vertical boxes with X-shaped dividers.

The desk unit below the storage wall includes two spacious bins at either end with hinged lids for easy access to materials. Marking and measuring devices are handy, yet out of the way in the large desk drawer.

The plywood couch incorporates two drawers under the seat for additional storage while providing a comfy place to relax. The end tables also serve double-duty in that they conceal two more large bins.
Plan #50345

4 STORAGE WALL: This elegant set of shelves is adaptable to any decor. While relieving the clutter caused by books and magazines scattered about on end tables and coffee tables, this unit also serves as a focal point for any room grouping. Its exquisite detailing and classic symmetry make it a masterpiece of originality. This one, unified setting displays and also conveniently conceals the many items a family needs and enjoys every day. The unique display section keeps a careful balance between bookshelves and display space. Plan #50130

5 FAMILY ROOM SHELVING SYSTEM: Pattern a family room wall with functional modules of storage spaces. Books, bric-a-brac, collector items — all add decorative interest to the wall. Doors cover some areas for handy concealed storage of less picturesque items. The unit can be divided into areas appropriate to whatever items and books you wish to display. Drawers may be used for anything from crayons, to craft supplies, to miniature race cars. The chalkboard at one end of the unit provides a play area for the kids or a special aid in helping with homework. Construction is well within the range of home shops, tools and carpentry skills. Get your family room organized with this efficient, yet versatile shelving system. Plan #50028

6 ARCHED BOOKCASE UNITS: Under the arches of this storage wall there's room for a display of books and accessories. The base cabinet supplies hidden space for records, toys and games. This easy-to-assemble project incorporates plywood for the arches and stock louvered doors. You can use a mellow stain to finish the unit, or create a truly customized version by painting it to complement the decor of your room. Add a dimensional effect by employing a cloth or wallpaper backing behind the shelves. Another option would be to cover the arched pieces with either fabric or a smashing wallpaper. Instead of the louvered doors, try fabric-insert shutters. Plan #50029

7 CONTEMPORARY STORAGE SYSTEM:
This brightly painted unit is precisely divided storage cubicles. Edging and framing are 1 × 12 pine; back and doors are 1/4 inch hardboard; and shelves and dividers are 3/8 inch particleboard. Plan and place colors for the most striking effect. Plan #50151

8 SLEEK STORAGE WALL: This carefully planned design provides room for a component system and a desk area plus lots of storage and display space. It's artfully designed to look beautiful and give you room to display your finest accessories, books and art objects. This wall is just a series of plywood boxes which you can put together in several components, arrange against the wall and fasten in place. Plan #50091

Bookcases/Wall Units 89

SHEER COMFORT

TUB/SHOWER DIVERTERS

When you go through your morning or evening ritual of turning on the shower and stepping into the tub, you expect the shower to work. But someday, something might go wrong with its diverter — a device that directs the flow of water to the shower head. Fortunately, however, you can troubleshoot and correct such problems with a minimum amount of tools and hassles.

Tub/shower diverters fall into two general classifications. Those of one group, called stem valve diverters, are housed in the faucet body and direct the flow of water from there. Tub diverter spouts, on the other hand, act independently of the faucet. Diverter mechanisms vary but they all do the same thing. In the closed position, the diverter valve blocks off the water flow to the shower head. Opened fully, it routes incoming water to the shower head.

With certain tub diverter spouts, lifting up on the knob while the water is running seals off the inlet to the spout and forces the water up to and out of the shower head. The water pressure will maintain the seal. When the water is shut off, the knob will drop back into its usual position.

When a tub diverter spout wears out, or if the lift rod attached to the knob breaks off from the plate it is attached to, you may as well replace the spout. To remove the defective one, insert a hammer handle or another suitable item into the spout and rotate it counter-clockwise until it separates from the nipple it is attached to. Wrap pipe compound or tape around the nipple and install the new spout.

If a stem valve begins to leak or no longer will divert water properly, shut off the water supply to the faucet, drain the lines and remove the nut holding the stem in place. Withdraw the stem, inspect the packing washer or O ring and the seat washer, if your diverter has one, and replace any worn-out parts.

1 BEDSIDE HELPER: This roll-about bed stand sports a drop-leaf extension that can be flipped up when you need a bed tray. Use it as a convenient nightstand, and then roll it out when you want to have breakfast in bed and browse through the Sunday paper. Plan #50442

Bed and Bath 91

2

92 Bed and Bath

2 DAYBED: This handsome and serviceable daybed is 30 inches high, 81 inches long, and 35 1/2 inches wide. It's a great place to lounge during the day, but at night a single mattress turns it into an extra bed if you need one. Just the thing for guests in a home without a guest room. Plan #50256

3 HERITAGE HOPE CHEST: This 2 × 4 × 1 1/2-foot-high storage chest can double as a sturdy bench. The top and front are decorated with a unique double butterfly design. Wood plugs conceal the recessed bolts that hold the chest together. Plan #50428

4 BATHROOM PROJECTS: This one plan includes vanity, mirror frame, light fixture, and the wall cabinet. The walls are paneled with exterior grade fir plywood treated with exterior stain. The see-through towel rack and shelf are made of clear acrylic. It's a complete yet inexpensive way to redecorate your bath. Plan #50341

5 LAVATORY COUNTER: Here's a renewal project that can improve almost any bathroom. It will give you more counter, shelf and drawer space, and more grooming room than you've ever had before. The counter and cabinet unit measures 5$1/2$ feet altogether; the unit above the tank adds another 2$1/2$ feet to the length. Build from plywood and paint or stain. Plan #50014

6 SHELF/CABINET SYSTEM: This shallow unit doesn't take much floor space, but it does a big storage job. It projects just four inches from the wall unit until it clears the door area, then extends to six or eight inches over the tub, depending on the space limitations. The overhead cabinets are 10 inches deep. Plan #50105

7 LINEN CLOSET: Utilize every inch of space by building this linen closet into an existing closet or as a freestanding unit. Pull-out trays and deep shelving are designed for specialized storage. Drawers conceal table linens and out-of-season bedding. Plan #50114

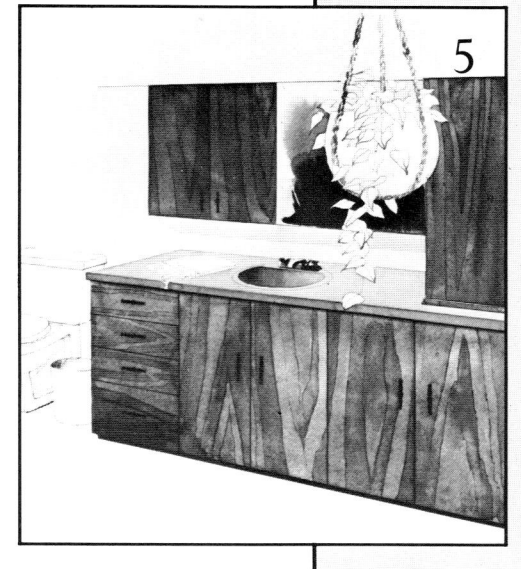

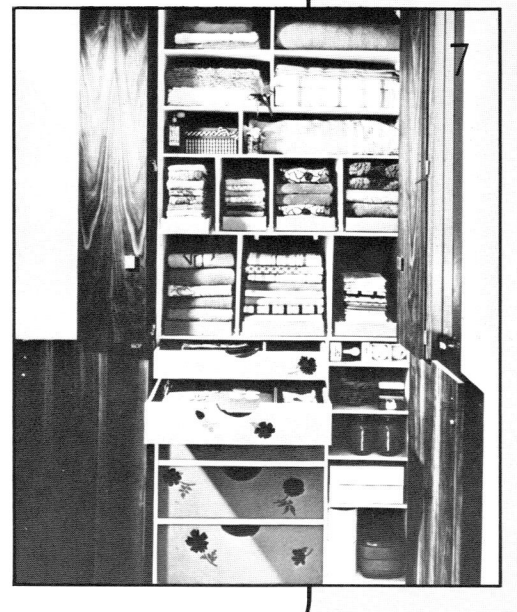

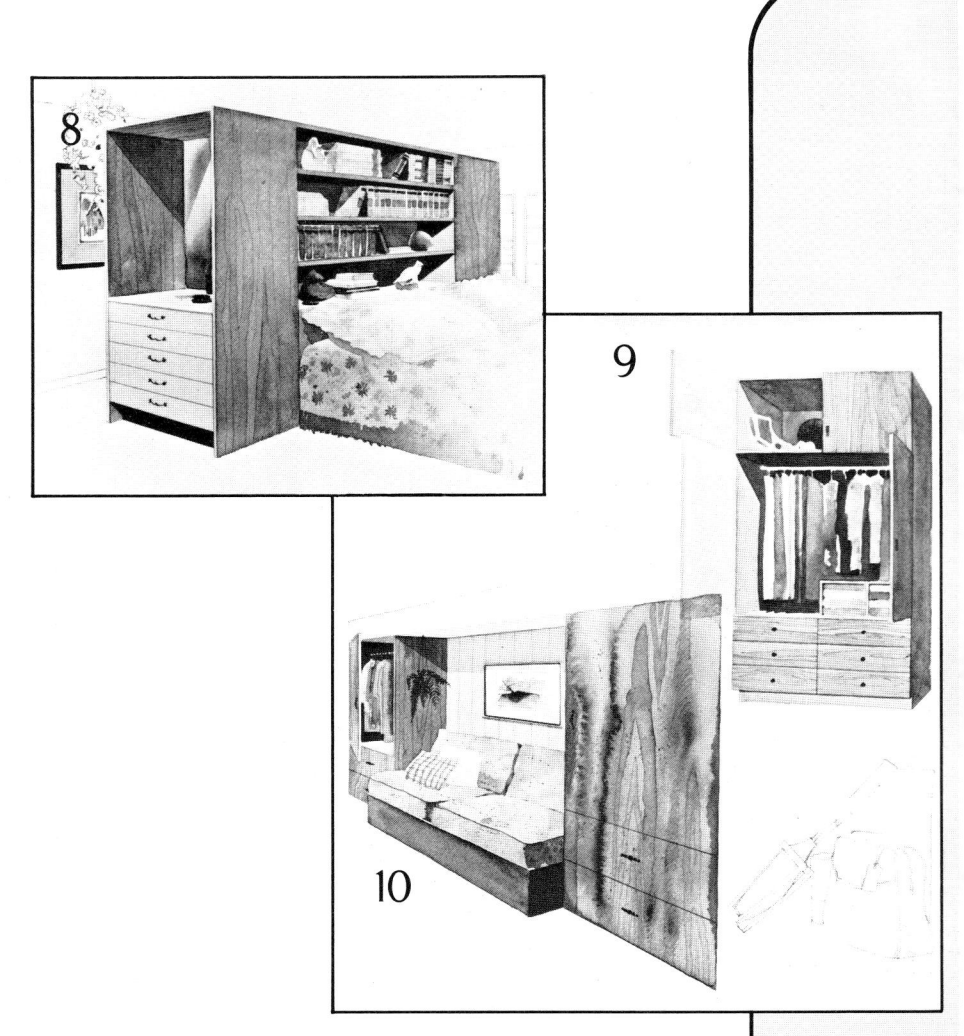

8 DOUBLE HEADBOARD: Gain extra storage space with this unit which features individual dressers at either end and two closets behind with 5 feet of hanging space. Plan #50274

9 BIG WARDROBE: This tailor-made closet is the perfect way to keep all his things separate from hers in an organized fashion. Central storage compartments allow maximum hanging space, yet leave room for six drawers and a deep shelf above and below. Plan #50164

10 SLEEP/STORAGE ALCOVE: Closets flank a built-in daybed to create a bedroom that does double-duty. Perfect for a small bedroom or as an addition to a den or study. Plan #50162

96 Bed and Bath

11 VANITY/WARDROBE WALL: Because it is only 12 feet long and 2 feet wide, this unit frees floor space in the bedroom plus adding storage. Each closet hold two closet poles for hanging clothes, while seven drawers beneath the vanity offer generous space for foldable items. A flip-up mirror reveals the compartment for cosmetics. Plan #50166

12 CLEVER CLOSET ORGANIZER: By opening up the wall of a double closet from floor to ceiling, you can substitute this well-organized garment center; it's complete with shelves and drawers for shoes and accessories. Space that was formerly between the clothespole and the ceiling has been transformed into two long shelves that can be closed off with swing-out doors. Plan #50026

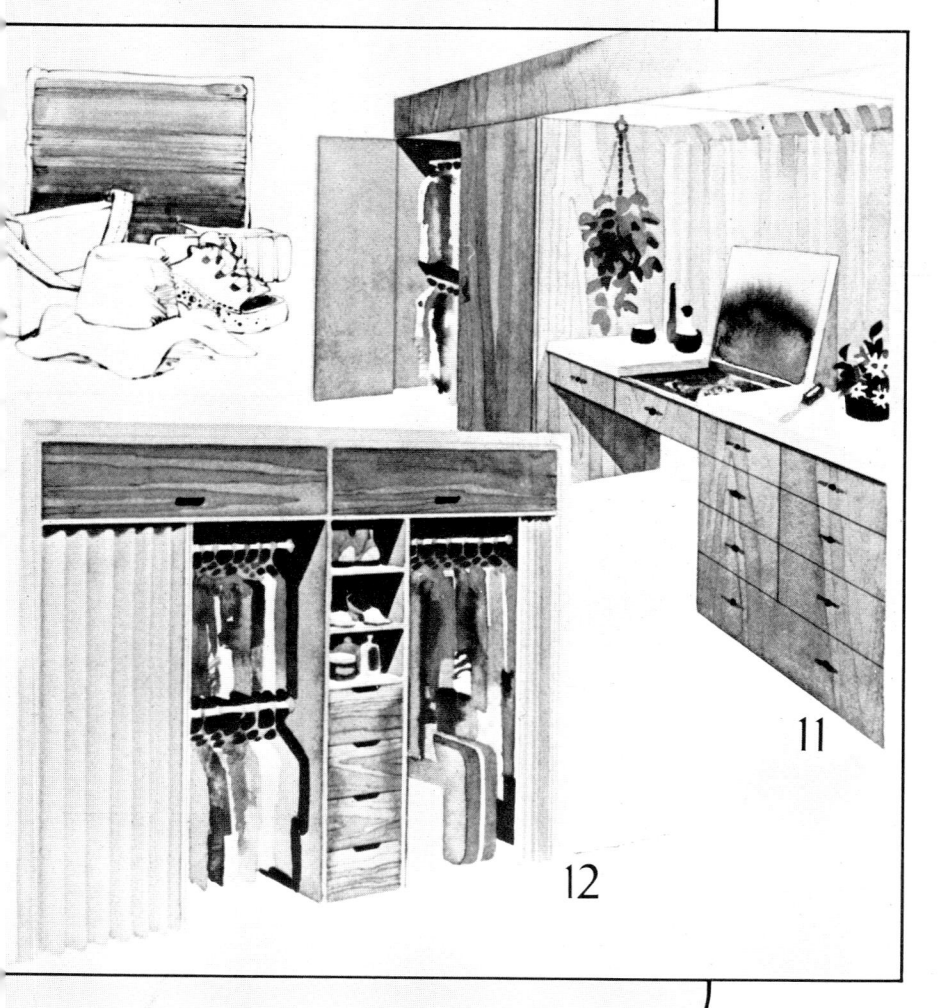

MEASURING FOR SHADES AND SUCH

You've undoubtedly noticed that shutters, mini-slat Venetian blinds and shades of all kinds have become popular alternatives to conventional drapery and curtain treatments. The vertical Mylar blinds used in the family entertainment center featured on the next few pages adds a distinctive touch to the overall neutral color scheme. Although installing blinds and shutters is slightly trickier than hanging draperies, you can make the job easier by getting accurate window measurements before ordering materials.

Window shades can be easily mounted inside or outside the casing — the decision is up to you. To fit the shades inside the casing, measure the top of the window from one inside edge of the frame to the other — this will give you your "tip-to-tip in-box" measurement. Provide this measurement when ordering and specify you want an allowance made for brackets. To determine length, measure the window opening top to bottom and order your shade at least eight inches longer.

When shades are installed outside the casing, the brackets are usually mounted in the center of the trim. Measure between these two points to determine shade width. For length, measure from the middle of the top casing to the sill and plan for an additional eight inches of window shade.

To hang Venetian blinds inside the casing, you'll need at least one inch of flat surface on the inside of the trim to attach the brackets. To determine width, measure between the points where the brackets will be placed. For length, measure from the inside top edge of the casing down to the windowsill.

Shutters may be hung inside or outside the window casing, but fit is more critical when installed inside the casing. For inside-mounted panels and ensembles, measure across the top, middle, and bottom of the window area. Use the widest of the three measurements and subtract $1/8''$ for each panel in a row to allow for hinge spacing. To determine length, measure the window at left, center, and right from top to bottom inside the casing. Use the longest measurement. For full window length, subtract $1/4''$ to clear the top and bottom of the sill. For cafe shutters, divide the window height by two and add two inches.

1 CRAFT CENTER/BAR/PIANO COVE: Located along one wall of this total entertainment center is the activity area. The crafts center features a fold-down, laminated work surface and plenty of storage space. The bar and refreshment storage section swivels out of sight when not in use, and there's a small sink area — enlarged with mirrors — that contains built-in wine storage. Plan #50221

Entertainment Room 99

100 Entertainment Room

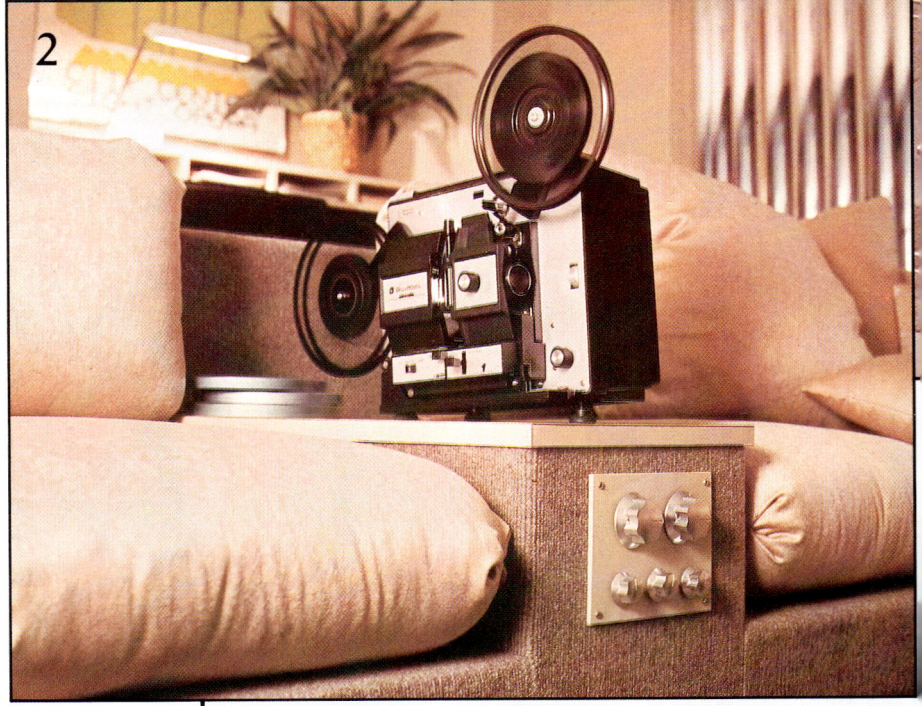

2 SEATING PLATFORM: The central, carpet-covered seating platform unifies this comfortable, well organized room. The carpet, which also covers the floor and one wall, serves to soften the sound level when lots is happening all at once. One section of the seating platform houses the movie projector storage/audio control panel for easy access when viewing home movies or more extensive projects. When you're in the mood for a movie, simply lift the lid, lift out the projector, and start the reels rolling. The easy-care cushions are zippered and covered with drip-dry fabric cases. Plan #50223

3

3 SEWING & ENTERTAINMENT CENTER:
This center includes a complete sewing area with a fold-down table, lots of storage and a niche for a dress form. There's space for your video equipment and plenty of room for game storage. The all-in-one audio center has been designed with special compartments for albums, tapes, stereo accessories and a tape deck. The speakers for this room's four-channel sound system have been evenly spaced around the room for best sound reproduction. Plan #50222

1 COFFEE TABLE COMPONENTS: This compact unit features record storage on one side with the cassette player, amplifier and turntable recessed in the top. With the sliding smoked-plastic dust covers closed, the table serves a bevy of floor sitters. It's just the thing for small room with little wall area. Plan #50231

2

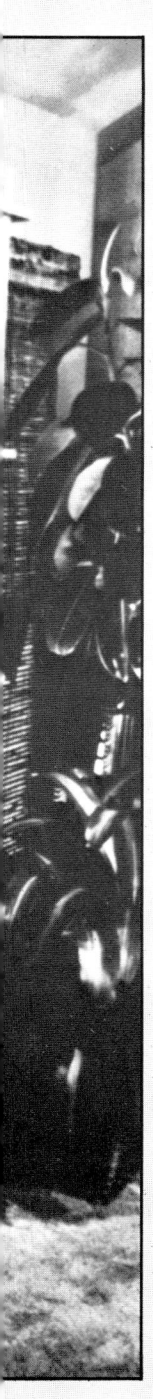

2 SUPER SIMPLE STORAGE: Any room of your house would function more efficiently with this build-it-yourself storage and entertainment center. It's versatile enough to serve as a bookshelf, game center or display unit for plants, china, whatever you love to show off.

Because of its size, 7 feet wide × 7½ feet high × 18 inches deep, this unit could easily become a focal point in a room. The plan even comes with an additional table and some stools which tuck away along the bottom two shelves. The table, stored directly under the stereo component section, has a hinged top which fits over the base when it's opened. Each stool consists of a four-inch plywood box atop a crosswork base; cushions add comfort and decorative appeal.

To construct the unit, cut notches in the four vertical panels and then cut notches and drill holes for the dowels in the shelves. Insert dowels in the shelves on both sides of the uprights to stabilize the unit and keep horizontals from slipping. When you put the unit together, lay it down on the floor and enlist a helper.

This storage/entertainment center is good-looking "as is," but you might want to stain or paint it to complement the color scheme and decor of your room. Plan #50337

3 RECORD STORAGE CUBE: This cube table record keeper is an attractive accessory, but pull out the front and there's a roomy drawer for storing a whole record collection, all partitioned for various types of albums. It's easy to build from fir plywood covered with bright plastic laminate. Plan #50115

4 STEREO CABINET: Protect your audio equipment inside this elegantly designed cabinet. Glass doors keep the dust from getting into delicate electronic gear as well as protecting it from curious children or active pets. The tasteful styling is at home in any room and complements any decor or style of furniture. Plan #50429

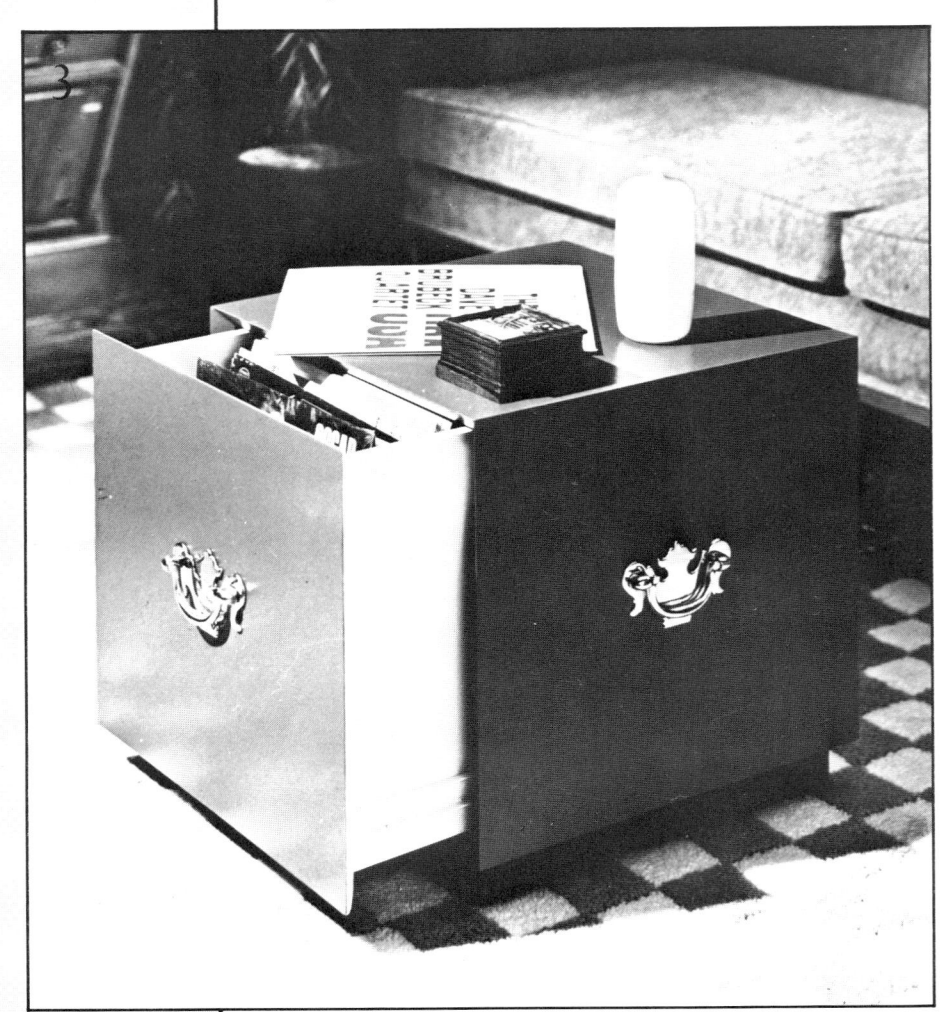

4

Component Units 107

5 PEDESTAL TELEVISION CABINET: The top section of this cabinet houses a one-touch, solid-state portable color television. The bottom half offers ample space for those hard-to-store over-scale books. Plan #50233

108 Component Units

6 WALL-HUNG TAPE STORAGE: This project provides a shelf for your tape deck as well as a fold-down rack which holds tapes at an angle so titles are easy to read. Extra storage is tucked behind the tapes. Plan #50230

Component Units 109

110 Component Units

7 CHAIRSIDE RECORDER: This table doubles as a self-contained record player and storage unit. The sides are decorated with geometric panels which disguise two swing-out lid supports. Even when open there's still plenty of table-top space left. Plan #50232

8 COMPONENT AND RECORD STORAGE: This simple box houses a tape deck, stereo receiver and turntable, with plenty of room for all those records. Plan #50229

Component Units 111

9

9 STORAGE AND ENTERTAINMENT WALL: A perfect working unit for a busy family room or the perfect complement to a more formal living room, this shelving unit adds a graceful note of beauty to your home. It's equipped to organize a hodgepodge of belongings, including books, television set and video equipment plus all your audio gear and accessories. There's even room for your family's games and toys.

Simply constructed from rough-cut redwood plywood, its appearance is one of practicality and durability. If you want to achieve a more formal style, you can build the unit from walnut or oak veneer.

The numerous display shelves of this unit are easily adjustable so that you can accommodate those outsized art and photography books or even tall vases complete with exotic dried flower arrangements.

Interesting effects can be created by rearranging the shelving units to complement other alterations you might make in the room. Leave one section devoid of shelves and hang photographs or prints and then highlight them with simple clip-on lights.

Each of the drawers is saw marked to look like two. In the bottom compartments, you can store a multitude of craft supplies, extra party gear, or your record collection. Plan #50111

SIZING UP UPHOLSTERED FURNITURE

A sofa or upholstered chair is a major investment that should pay off in many years of service. To help you choose wisely, here are some important aspects of construction that you should check when you consider such an investment.

To check the construction of a chair, ask to have it turned upside down. Quality frames are made of seasoned kiln-dried hardwood, such as ash, birch, hackberry, oak, maple or elm. The highest quality wooden frames are constructed of an interlocking assembly of pieces. Two pieces, for example, will be cut and fitted together like the pieces of a jigsaw puzzle, rather than butted up against each other. Good furniture also may be joined by spiral groove dowels or double dowels. Corner blocks should be screwed and glued.

Quality furniture has lots of coils covering the platform, while inferior furniture has fewer coils placed farther apart. The best construction consists of springs that are hand-tied in several directions — front to back, side to side, and across two diagonals. Springs in the back should of the same construction, but will be lighter weight.

In the next stage of construction, a sheet of burlap or other fabric is placed on top of the springs to separate them from the filling material. Better quality furniture has two or three layers of filling placed on top of the burlap. Cotton, natural or rubberized interlaced hair, foam rubber, and urethane foam are good padding materials.

Check the hangtags for fiber content of fabrics. Often, more than one fiber is used to take advantage of the best qualities of each. Cotton or rayon may be woven with other fibers to increase absorbency. Also, both cotton and rayon take dyes well. Acrylics can improve softness. Nylon and olefin add strength and cleanability. Acetate may be included for added luster, and polyester for easy cleaning.

Your budget, of course, will determine what you actually buy, but inspect for quality and always buy the best you can afford.

ORIENTAL ROOM: If you have a room you've been waiting to work on, how about turning it into a relaxing retreat with contemporary styling that incorporates Oriental characteristics. This plan contains all the necessary pieces for creating your own Eastern tranquility. Plan #50243

Oriental Room 115

116 Oriental Room

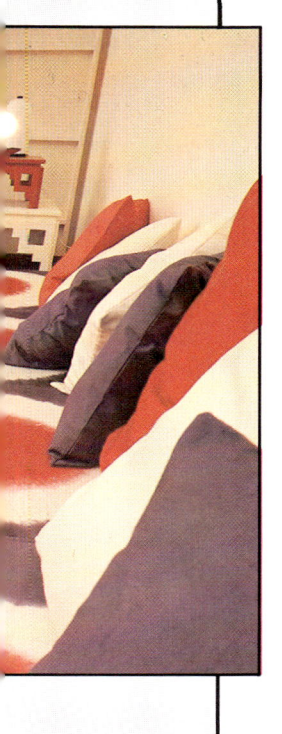

1 PLATE RACK: Adding vertical interest and accented by simply designed plates, this plate rack is a practical decorating addition to any room. Plan #50243

2 SEATING PLATFORM: This modular seating platform can be arranged to complement the other furniture in any room and yet accommodate even a large party. The cushions and loose pillows offer a comfortable and inviting area for relaxing. Plan #50243

3 SCREENS: In Japan, such screens are often used as wintertime windows — admitting light, but keeping out drafts. Covered in muslin, they may be decorated to accent your home's decor. Plan #50243

4 THREE TABLES: These versatile tables are functional as well as practical in their approach to providing areas for display of your most cherished treasures or for lamps. Plan #50243

Oriental Room 117

1

2

1 LOVESEAT: This soft and easy loveseat basically incorporates a box design which is covered with four plump pillows. The pillows are made so that they slip over the wood slat back for a snug fit. Plan #50360

2 PLYWOOD CONTOUR CHAIR: Sit back and relax in this chair that's made of 3/4-inch plywood, upholstery webbing and a super-soft pad that molds to its undulating shape. Front, sides and back are of plywood — sanded, primed and enameled. Rope and upholstery webbing keep the pad from sagging under body weight. Easy to make, this chair employs simple butt-joint construction. The upholstery is made in much the same way as stuffing a pillow. Plan #50310

3 SUNBURST EASY CHAIR: This dramatic chair is one of our most challenging projects, but it's worth the extra effort. Cut a series of tapered slats for the side on a table saw and joint them to a circle to form a fan shape. Apply molding to the outer edges and span them with seat and back. A distinctive wood, like poplar, will highlight the design. Plan #50387

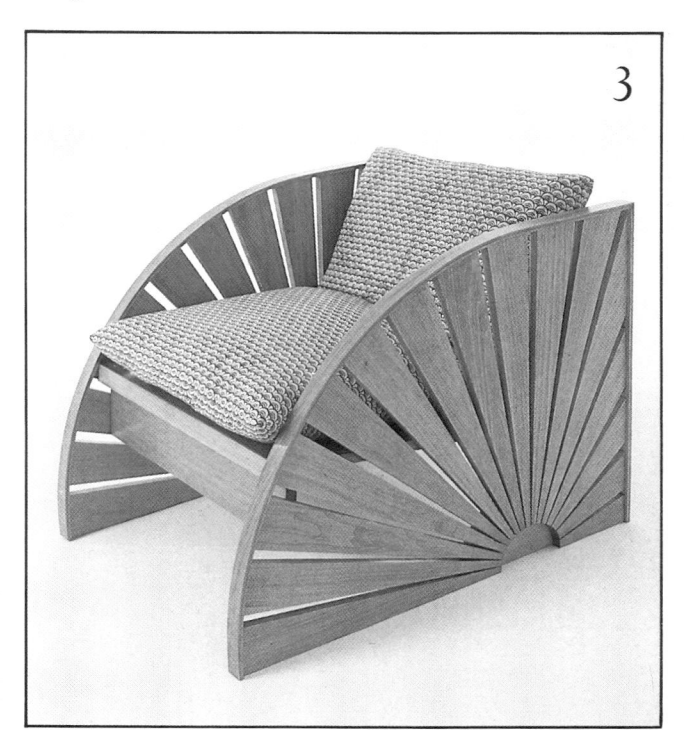

Seating Arrangements 119

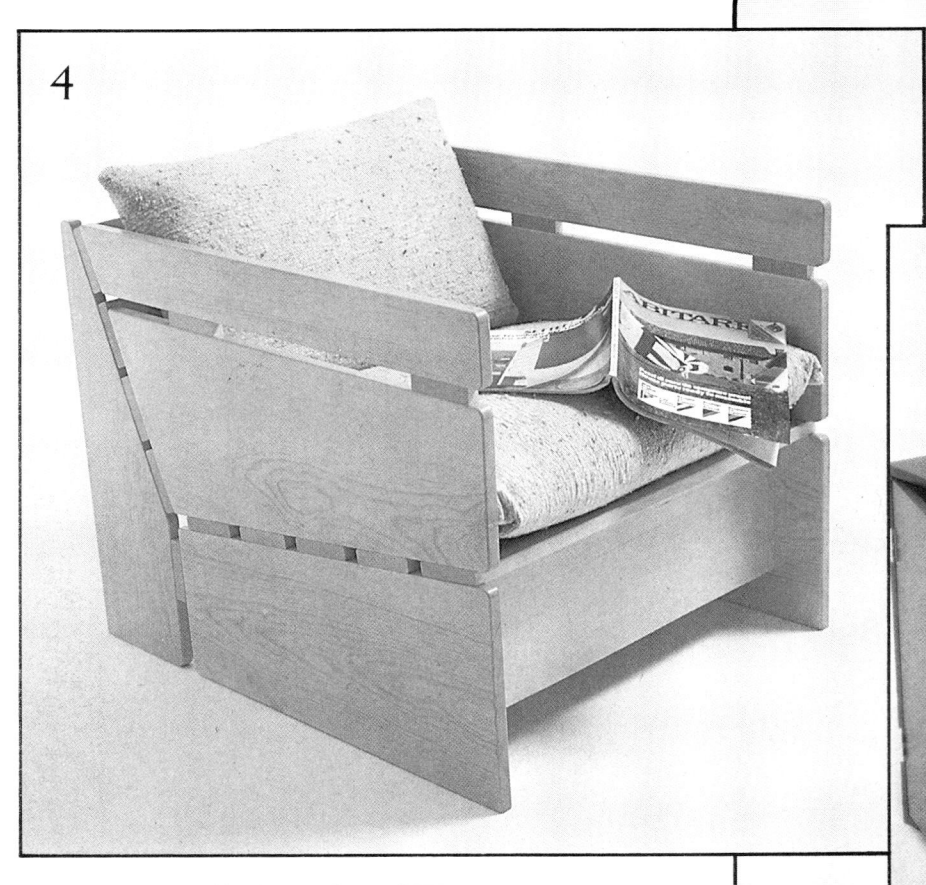

4 SLAT AND SLOT LOUNGER: Once you master ripping wood at an angle, you can put this comfortable chair together in a snap. Ripped 1 × 12s and 1 × 8s form the sides, and 1 × 4s the seat and back. For the lounge chair here, we used easy-to-shape pine and covered it with a protective coat of clear finish. Plan #50383

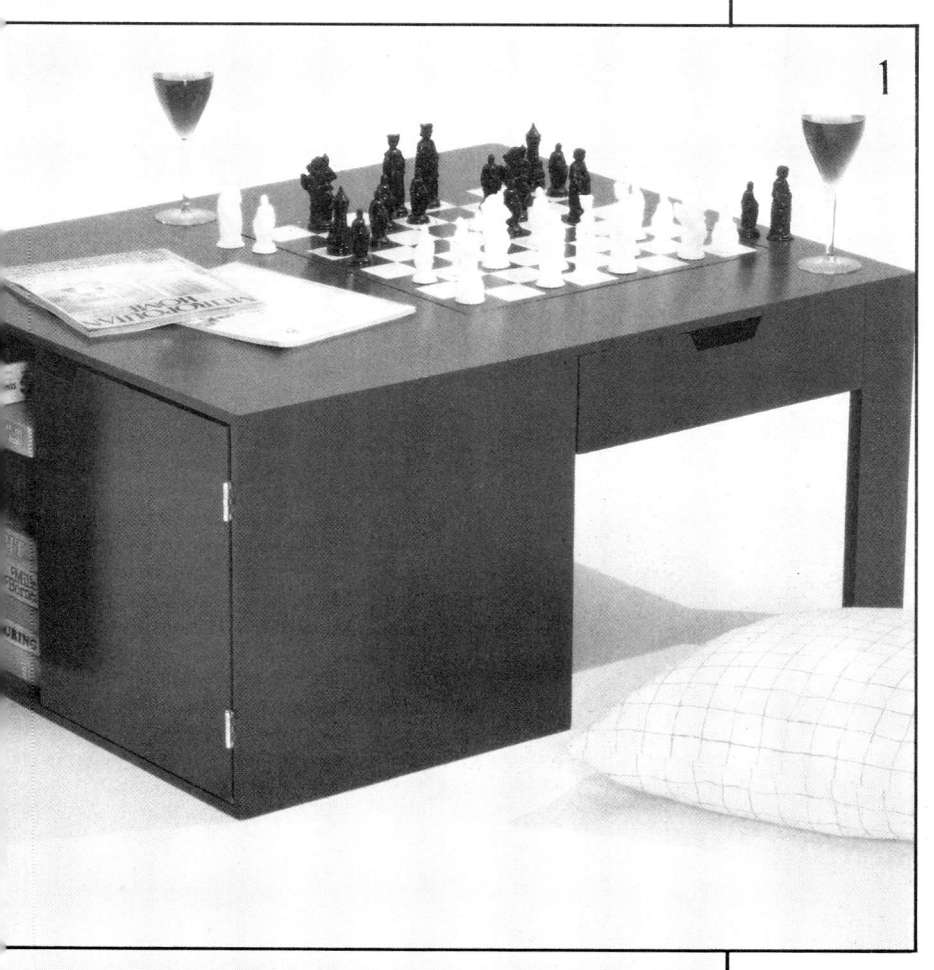

1 GAME-BOARD TABLE: Store all your games and puzzles in this 30 × 36 × 16-inch tall coffee table assembled from 1½ sheets of ½" plywood. The chess or checkerboard can be flipped over for a plain top if you wish. Plan #50431

2 COFFEE/DINING TABLE COMBO: Just flip up the base and our coffee table is ready for elegant dining. Build two four-sided boxes from 1/2-inch plywood: one measuring 22 × 28 × 14, the other 15 × 21 × 14 inches. Join them together with 1 × 4s nailed and glued to all edges. Use miter joints. Make the top from 3/4-inch birch plywood. Add a 1/4 × 2-inch strip to outer edges of surface to form recess for glass. Paint all pieces. Having glass cut to fit the recessed opening. Plan #50347

3 ART DECO LIGHTED TABLE: Add this uniquely attractive table to your living room decor. Geometrically layered legs give it the art decor flavor and the lighting recessed within the table adds distinctive highlights to any objects to which you wish to draw attention.
Plan #50407

4 COLLECTOR'S TABLE: Your treasured breakables will be on view and yet dust-free and protected in this glassed table with hinged top. It's the perfect answer for displaying pieces of value without taking the risk of breakage.
Plan #50443

Table Ideas 123

5

6

124 Table Ideas

5 GLASS-TOPPED GAME TABLE: Nicer looking than the standard card table and yet just as functional, this table is assembled from $3/4$-inch plywood and measures 36 inches square by 29 inches high. The top is $1/4$-inch plate glass recessed below the top edge. The entire unit is finished with clear varnish. Plan #50321

6 EXTRA ROOMY STORAGE CHEST: Store extra linens, napkins, coasters or even the good silver in this handsome chest built of $3/4$-inch birch plywood. The finished unit measures 48 inches long, by $17^{1}/_{4}$ inches deep, by 30 inches high. The doors and drawers have notches for leather pulls. Plan #50361

7 VERSATILE WOODEN WINDOW BENCH:
This is a very practical piece you can use in many ways: for extra seating, as a coffee table, a plant table. Built from a basic box, parquet flooring adds it's special appeal. Plan #50148

ORDERING INFORMATION

The Garlinghouse Company is pleased to re-issue these Better Homes and Gardens project plans. It is our hope that this publication will assist you in making your home both more efficient and more enjoyable.

1. ORDERS should include full payment.

2. CHECKS AND MONEY ORDERS should be made payable to: The Garlinghouse Company.

3. MASTERCARD AND VISA CREDIT CARDS may be used for orders of $20.00 or more. Be sure to include your credit card number, the expiration date and your signature. We cannot process your order without this information.

4. COST OF PLANS is $4.95 for any plan ordered.

5. SHIPPING AND HANDLING CHARGES are $1.75 for the first plan that you order and $.50 for each plan thereafter.

6. MAIL ORDERS TO:
Garlinghouse/BH&G Project Plans,
P.O. Box 10251,
Des Moines, IA 50336

7. CANADIAN ORDERS should include payment in U.S. currency.

Ship To:
Name _____
Street _____ Apt. No. _____
City _____ State _____ Zip _____
Signature _____

Payment: ☐ Check or Money Order
☐ MasterCard ☐ Visa
Card No. _____
Exp. Date _____ **No C.O.D. Orders**

Item No.	Description	Qnty.	Total	Shipping & Handling	Total

Garlinghouse/BH&G Project Plans   G12   Order Total _____
P.O. Box 10251   Iowa/Kansas Residents Add 4% Sales Tax _____
Des Moines, IA 50336   Total _____

Ship To:
Name _____
Street _____ Apt. No. _____
City _____ State _____ Zip _____
Signature _____

Payment: ☐ Check or Money Order
☐ MasterCard ☐ Visa
Card No. _____
Exp. Date _____ **No C.O.D. Orders**

Item No.	Description	Qnty.	Total	Shipping & Handling	Total

Garlinghouse/BH&G Project Plans   G12   Order Total _____
P.O. Box 10251   Iowa/Kansas Residents Add 4% Sales Tax _____
Des Moines, IA 50336   Total _____

Ship To:
Name _____
Street _____ Apt. No. _____
City _____ State _____ Zip _____
Signature _____

Payment: ☐ Check or Money Order
☐ MasterCard ☐ Visa
Card No. _____
Exp. Date _____ **No C.O.D. Orders**

Item No.	Description	Qnty.	Total	Shipping & Handling	Total

Garlinghouse/BH&G Project Plans   G12   Order Total _____
P.O. Box 10251   Iowa/Kansas Residents Add 4% Sales Tax _____
Des Moines, IA 50336   Total _____